Love Chronicles

LOVE MANIFESTING IN ALL FORMS
FROM HIS & HER PERSPECTIVE

Copyright @ 2021 Michelle Dowleyne
All rights reserved.
ISBN: 979-8-9851725-1-5

Author owns complete rights to this book and may be contracted in regards to distribution. Printed in the United States of America.

Library of Congress Cataloging-in-Publication Data

The copyright laws of the United States of America protect this book. No part of this publication may be reproduced or stored in a retrieval system for commercial gain or profit.

No part of this publication may be stored electronically or otherwise transmitted in any form or by any means (electronic, photocopy, recording) without written permission of the author except as provided by USA copyright law.

Scripture quotations are taken from the Holy Bible, New Living Translation (NIV), copyright © 1996, 2004, 2007, 2013, 2015 by Tyndale House Foundation.

Editing: SynergyEd Consulting/ synergyedconsulting.com
Graphics & Cover Design: MyAsia Reed- My Blessed Hands
glightcreations.com/ glightcreations@gmail.com

shero publishing

Published by: SHERO Publishing
getpublished@sheropublishing.com

S H E R O P U B L I S H I N G . C O M

Be it advised that all information within this literary work, HER STORY IS MY STORY-LOVE CHRONICLES, has been acknowledged to be the truthful account of each co-author. The authors are responsible for the content in their individual chapter and hold SHERO Publishing harmless for any legal action arising as a result of their participation in this publication.

W W W . M I C H E L L E D O W L E Y N E . C O M

TABLE OF CONTENTS

DEDICATION		4
INTRODUCTION		5

Co-Author Stories:

Aja Williams	*Journey to Self-Love & Self-Discovery*	8
Angelia Ross-Lincoln	*Hidden Scars*	20
Anthony Taylor	*Coached to Win, Mentored to Love*	34
Bennie T. Harris III	*Love Without Limits*	48
Cecilia Vandervall	*Never Alone*	60
Darius & Sonia Lowery Scott	*Making it Last Forever*	74
Dr. Contress M. Braxton	*The Age of 19?*	88
Gerly Sapphire Harris	*Love, Disability, & Acceptance*	102
La'Kenya Walter	*Unmasking Single Love*	116
La'Kisha Lacey	*Because He Unconditionally Loves ME*	130
Lashena Shields	*Not The Right Husband for Me*	144
Sandra Williams	*A Transitioning Walk Without YOU*	152
About the Visionary		168

Dedication

This book is dedicated to all who have ever *loved*, all who have ever sought *love,* and all who have ever lost *love.* Love is a delicate word and can mean so many things to so many people. I dedicated this book to my grandmother, who taught me the meaning of *love.*

To the SHERO Publishing staff; the amazing Book Coaches that worked with our Co-Author group weekly to support our book, to Coach Kimberly Perry Sanderlin and Marketing Director Camilla Moore.... Thank You!! Thank you to CEO Erica Perry Green and the entire SHERO Publishing Team for all your work, collaboration, and support to make this project a reality. Also, thank you to our amazing Book Cover Artist, MyAsia Reed. Your work is amazing.

To the Co-Authors, my new family: Thank You, Thank You, and Thank You for sharing a part of your life with us. Your stories will bless so many readers who are seeking the answer to love. May God continue to bless you and use you to be a shining light. You stepped out on faith to share your stories, know that others are learning, growing, and healing from each of you.

Introduction

Has *love* every caused you pain, hurt, sadness, mistrust or confusion? Has the *love* for another left a hole, years later, that seems to be without repair? Have you ever wondered if the battle for *love* impacts men as it does women? The 13 Co-Authors of **Love Chronicles: Love Manifesting In All Forms, From His & Her Perspectives** are here to boldly share their journeys and battles to win love, sustain love, grow healthy love, and mend from loves lost. Through the pages of each chapter, you will learn about the vast complexities of love, exhibited in all types of relations; from parental love or the lack thereof, to the love of a spouse, sibling love, the love for children or even love poured into us by a mentor, coach, or spiritual advisor. Love impacts us all greatly. Visionary Michelle Dowleyne prays that this book will serve to bridge relationship gaps, heal hurts and mend love lost, for it all starts with **LOVE!**

~Author Michelle Dowleyne

www.michelledowleyne.com

Co-Authors:
Aja Williams
Angelia Ross-Lincoln
Anthony Taylor
Bennie T. Harris III
Cecilia Vandervall
Darius & Sonia Lowery Scott
Dr. Contress M. Braxton
La'Kenya Walter
La'Kisha Lacey
Lashena Shields
Sandra Williams
Sapphire Harris (Gerly)

Visionary Michelle Dowleyne

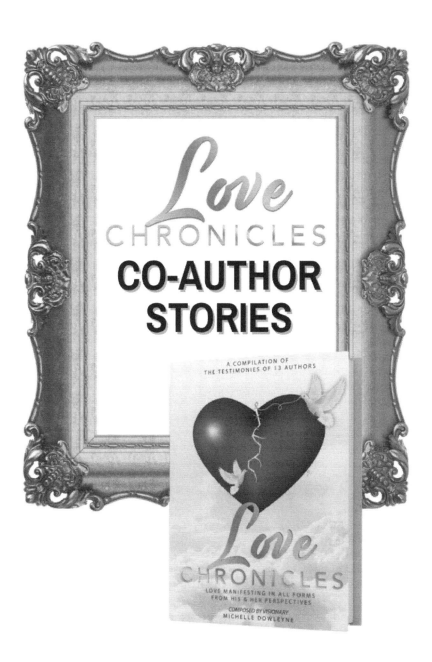

Author Aja Williams

Author Aja Williams

Aja H. Williams is from Boston, Massachusetts, and is a graduate of Regis College School of Nursing (Weston, Massachusetts) with a Bachelor of Science Degree in Nursing. She attended the University of Maryland School Of Nursing (Baltimore, Maryland) and graduated with a Master of Science in Community Public Health Nursing with a Certificate in Environmental Health Studies. Mrs. Williams has 12 plus years of clinical nursing experience in acute care, long-term care, and public/community-based settings. Prior to joining the Bureau of Health Workforce, at the Health Resources and Services Administration as a Nurse Consultant, she served as a Public Health Nurse Supervisor for the Department of Health and Human Services, Bureau of Clinical Services/Center Based Services for the Baltimore County Department of Health. She coordinated the nursing activities for the Reproductive Sexual Health (RSH) and Vaccines for Children (VFC) programs; to provide outreach and education that promotes healthy lifestyles, prevents diseases, and encourages early interventions and treatment services.

Her interests include traveling and spending time with family. Most recently, mindfulness and self-care practices sparked her interest.

Journey to Self-Love & Self-Discovery

"You are designed to reinvent and recreate yourself, over and over again."- Debbie Ford

Past

Everyone has their own journey to self-love and self-discovery. My journey started on September 20, 1985. I quote the day that I was born because self-love and self-discovery is a lifelong journey. Every day that I wake up I know there's a God-given purpose for my life and I imagine the things that I'm striving for. Before each year around the sun, I create a vision board, basically a visual representation of my goals, and at its core, my aspiration is to do all those things that make me happy. Most of us probably don't believe we need a formal definition of happiness; we know it when we feel it, it's often a term associated with positive emotions like joy, fulfillment, or love. I found that most researchers define happiness in the terms of "subjective wellbeing" or how satisfied you are with your life and being content with your progression towards your life's goals.

Let's use the example of my past. In the beginning, as far as I can remember, my childhood was great. I lived in a loving two-parent home. Both parents worked hard and did all they could to provide a structured environment. Then the hardships came. I can't recall exactly what age I was because I've resorted to suppressing those memories. However, I can remember the struggles: a tremendous amount of financial stress that included job loss and eviction and turmoil erupting in our household. Before this we lived comfortably; we were not rich but we certainly didn't struggle for our basic necessities. When that changed, it shaped the woman that I am today. I understand the many facets of poverty, from eviction to homelessness and being stripped away from the peace of a loving secure home, to depending on government assistance. I knew I was loved and cared for but these adverse childhood experiences left a lasting imprint on me. It made me feel like everything was yanked from under me, and I was left feeling vulnerable and like I couldn't count on the people around me to keep me safe.

As a little girl, I felt powerless and overwhelmed. As a result, I turned inward. As a form of denial and avoidance, I retreated and kept my feelings and emotions internal. I needed someone to help me make sense of what I was experiencing. I knew my parents weren't available emotionally, they were in survival mode, so they were unable to see what I was going through. Food became my emotional comfort, and isolation became my security blanket. I resorted to suppressing and hiding my feelings of anxiety, depression, stress, low self-esteem as long as I could. I did not know how to process it all then, but God has a way of turning your pain into purpose.

Most importantly, throughout my childhood years, God kept me and my family safe and together. Family and friends are important resources for support and comfort in both times of joy and distress. I'm thankful for those who stepped in when we needed them the most until our situation turned for the better. It has always been for those who invested in me: parents, family, and friends, that I studied hard to get good grades to graduate and establish a great career and reinvent my past. I felt that achieving success was my way of erasing every past hurtful memory. I was going to reclaim a legacy for my entire family. But what I soon learned was that I was developing people-pleasing behaviors, which can arise as a response to fear associated with trauma. If you've ever experienced trauma as a child, you may have learned it was safer to do what other people wanted and take care of their needs first. By people-pleasing first, you made yourself likable, and therefore safe. I can totally relate to this, I wanted to make those closest to me happy, which meant I became reluctant to open up when I was struggling; I only did so when I was on the brink of totally breaking down, or I was in isolation because I had held it all in for far too long. I knew I had to make a change and my journey to self-love and self-discovery allowed me to let go of who I thought I was supposed to be and embrace who I am today. I soon came to realize that from the moment we are born our parents and society play an important role in determining how we see the world. However, it's not until we let go of these taught assumptions that we propel towards our greatness that lies within.

Also, continuing on the path of hiding behind a huge smile, people-pleasing, failure to say no, in order to avoid conflict led me to no boundaries and hitting a brick wall. This led to full depletion. I had nothing to give, no energy, and no purpose. I couldn't keep up a façade any longer. The hardest lesson from my past was that I had to realize that my parents were humans and they were trying to do the best that they could with what they knew. As I got older I started to see how hard it was for them. I gained compassion because I knew they did the best they could with what they had. From that point on, I chose to own my story, to be brave standing in my truth, and to make every attempt to perfect the three key core values my parents always instilled in me, which are faith (Keep God first), respect (Treat all people with dignity), and responsibility (Work hard for what you want in life). I intended to live a life worth living.

Marriage

In early adulthood, I thought my life was great, everything appeared normal on the outside. I graduated college, left the nest to move to another state to start my career. I had no residual symptoms of the past I once knew. Then, as an adult, something triggered all the emotional baggage I thought I had buried years ago. I discovered that I was still healing from my past hurt and it impacted my way of thinking and relating to the world and others as an adult.

In my late 20's I found the love of my life. We got married, we traveled often, purchased our first home and everything was pure bliss. But eventually, in my marriage, that emotional baggage crept in. I looked to my spouse to make me feel secure and happy with myself. I had some self-esteem issues and the little girl in me resurfaced. There was this longing to be seen, acknowledged, and protected all the time. This led me to explore my past again, particularly my relationship with my dad. I once heard Iyanla Vanzant say a father's role in a daughter's life is to teach a girl how to be with herself as a woman and how to have a nonsexual but intimate relationship with men. My dad was around most of my life, but I still felt "daddy-less" because he wasn't present. I wanted to hear from him that I was beautiful, or whatever adjective he wanted to use to describe how perfect I was in his eyes. This longing made me search for validation from others. I wanted my husband to fill that void. I unfairly pushed unspoken expectations on him. I made him feel like nothing he did was good enough. I grew resentful because I pushed the responsibility on him to make me feel happy, beautiful, and worthy of love.

I was insecure about everything; I would push my husband away through my words and actions because I didn't feel deserving of his support and love. I hadn't felt safe or cradled by my earliest childhood experiences with adults, so my sense of security was flawed. I relied on what I knew best; once again *food became my emotional comfort and isolation became my security blanket*. I then took a wrong turn towards seeking self-love and self-discovery through the world. I became immersed in self-help books, social media, horoscopes, and modeling others' behaviors. I was desperately exploring and seeking to understand what my God-given purpose is on this planet.

I was troubled and lost, confused about who I was as a woman. I had no sense of how I should show up in the world or why I was here in the first place. So when I received the gift to become a mom I didn't think I was going to be able to be a good mom because I didn't think I was worthy of that amount of love.

Present- New baby

All I knew about mothering and womanhood was what I learned from my mother. She was a survivor, strong, hardworking, selfless, and giving to others all the time, even when she didn't have much to give. I always say- *she pours from an empty cup*. I don't choose to live that way. I want to fill my cup first, and *"may my cup runneth over"* (Psalm 23:5) so that I have more than enough for my needs. I want to be able to pour out to others from my overflow. Michelle Obama said "I want my daughters to see a mother who loves them dearly, who invests in them, but who also invests in herself. It's just as much about letting them know as young women that it is okay to put yourself a little higher on your priority list."

I would say that my daughter opened up my heart and being a mother has helped me flourish into the woman God wants me to be. I want my daughter to see me fulfilled. I want to teach her that by neglecting yourself, you run the risk of not being your best self. And if I'm not the best version of myself, I become resentful, irritable, and dissatisfied with myself. I risk developing poor health, and not being able to pursue my goals, and ultimately my family suffers. So I think of the phrase- *"you simply can't pour from an empty cup."* It is factual. Having a daughter has allowed me to rebirth myself into a woman of God. I strive more to be the best version of myself; to be a positive example in my daughter's life.

Health/Mental/Loss of Identity

After having a baby, there was a time when I didn't feel like myself and was losing the sense of who I was. Where's my joy? Who am I? I felt like I was failing at being a wife and a mother and I found myself having an episodic mental breakdown. I was tearful, seeking my healthcare provider's help. I told no one about this, for I was too ashamed. My healthcare provider referred me to a psychiatrist and prescribed antidepressant meds and therapy. I humbly accepted therapy because I wanted to get to the root of what was causing me to feel like I was losing control and feeling no sense of purpose. I tried several therapists before I found the one I had a soul connection with.

I'm grateful for therapy. The tools I learned have shaped my paradigm shift. I was once ashamed. I am no longer. What my therapist has taught me has led to my journey of self-discovery. The process of self-discovery has led me to learn who I am in God and his purpose for my life. Sometimes motherhood teaches us how to love unselfishly and grow to be the best version of ourselves, but first we, mothers, have to learn to mother ourselves.

Future

My Purpose Statement-
To be a light of courage and fortitude and resilience; to continue to walk a path of healing

Next Five Years of My Life

Over the last year, during the pandemic, I have been in my own personal isolation/quarantine for healing and protecting my peace. The pandemic has literally allowed me to slow down and shut out the fear-based opinions that I was allowing myself to indulge in. Instead, I sit in my truth, focusing on affirming and believing in the power of God to heal and protect. I give up control of feeding into the assumptions of who I think I should be. There is no timeline;

self-discovery is lifelong. Each day I wake up, I know there is still a God-given purpose for my life. So I am determined not to waste a minute; I'm choosing to be brave, I'm choosing to own my story, and I'm choosing to love myself. Every single trial and tribulation has led me to this point in time. What I've learned is that you must heal from the burdens that weigh you down and prevent you from experiencing true freedom and happiness and self-love. We must believe it is our God-given right to live a life worth living and fly high because we are all worthy of love and happiness. I am just tapping into my power as a woman, wife, and mother, but I am so much more. I am loving the person who I am becoming on this path of self-love and self-discovery.

Love Notes:

Author Angelia Ross-Lincoln

Author Angelia Ross-Lincoln

Angelia Ross-Lincoln was born in Bainbridge, Georgia in 1975 to Henrietta Carter. For the past couple of years, Angelia has been living in Charleston, SC. She has two sons whom she loves and adores and a grandbaby who has literally stolen her heart. Angelia works for Charleston County School District as a Behavior Interventionist. She describes her job *"as living a dream."*

Angelia has a passion for helping at-risk children and a heart to do the same. Angelia personally faced the loss of her oldest son, who was killed in 2017 and dealt with a painful divorce. These incidents caused Angelia to be consumed by grief, depression, and suicide attempts; but God had a greater calling on her life. Due to her personal journey, Angelia is always talking and speaking to groups of other grieving mothers and women dealing with painful divorces about their *love loss* and how to manage grief and find love within themselves on a day-to-day basis.

Angelia has always had a passion to help others and has been quoted as being a dynamic speaker on several occasions. She desires to, one day, become a household name in a way that people know who she is and embrace the presence that she brings.

Angelia finally started believing in herself and realized God had a higher calling on her life. She went back to school and obtained her Associates Degree in Criminal Justice, then continued on to earn her Bachelor of Science Degree in Management with a concentration in Business. She is now pursuing her Masters in Management. Angelia still has the desire to one day become a Life Coach and to help and encourage other women that no matter what they are going through, whether it's depression, grief, insecurities, not feeling like enough, abuse (emotional or physical), they too can overcome it all. With all that she has been through, Angelia still chose to live life on the happy side and wants others to know that they can too.

Once you read Angelia's story and the trials and tribulations that she has endured since the age of 18, you will wonder how she finds the strength to even breathe! How was she able to find love again? Who was the wind beneath her wings? Angelia knows her life is not her own and that the Most-High uses her as a vessel.

When she's not working, Angelia enjoys arts and crafts, traveling, watching tv, and spending time with family and friends. Her motto is *"I Pray That Everything I Want I Will Achieve."*

Angelia dedicates her chapter to her son, the one individual who saved her, Amari Jamir Ross.

Hidden Scars

I used to dream big as a little girl; I would sit and wonder, how did the rich get rich. Growing up, I always wanted the pretty things in life, the flashy stuff I saw others with, but who didn't. I just didn't know what I had to do to get it. Growing up in the projects like I did was a badge of honor. Although when it was time to leave I was ready. Acceptance to college provided me a way out. It also provided me with a reality check. I soon discovered that I wasn't fully prepared like my friends and classmates for college life on my own. Even life in the projects had not prepared me with any clues to handle the many challenges of life that came my way. Little did I know my first real love would tragically be taken away from me in a blink of an eye. As cliché as it may sound, but as true as it is- "You never know how strong you are until being strong is the only choice you have." This is my story.

Meeting people was not hard for me. However, in college, I was around so many smart students that I did feel as if I was out of my element. Nevertheless, I kept telling myself, "I got this." I would see the students in my apartment complex having what looked like fun; drinking and smoking weed, and yes, curiosity got the best of me. So one Sunday evening I was invited down to a party. I was told it was Super Bowl Sunday and the biggest football game of the year was being played, so people usually party. I was only 18 years old and wasn't a football fan, but hey, the students liked me. They had invited me and I was going. After being at the party for an hour or so, I was offered a drink. Yes, it was an alcoholic drink in the form of a mixed drink. After a few of them, I stopped tasting the alcohol; the drinks were so delicious! I knew I was beginning to get intoxicated. Yet, instead of going back to my apartment, I chose to stay and drink even more. Biggest mistake of my life to that point! I later woke up having had what I thought was a bad dream.

I got up to use the bathroom because, in the dream, I thought I was urinating on myself. As I got up, I realized I was back in my own apartment. How did I get from the party back to my apartment? I was moving slowly and my body was in pain. Why did I feel as if I had been hit by a truck? As I made my way to the bathroom, I noticed something else. Where did all the blood come from? Slowly, I was starting to make sense of the dream and everything that had occurred. It was evident that it hadn't been a dream! I had been raped! I didn't know who raped me. I didn't know how many raped me. I didn't know where the rape occurred. All I knew was that I needed to go to the hospital, but was too embarrassed to go, so I didn't. In fact, from that point, I didn't go anywhere anymore.

I shut down and withdrew. I did not go to school or work; I went nowhere. I felt like I was, for a lack of better words, a complete slut. I quit everything. I no longer had the motivation to move on, so I found myself a college dropout and homeless. Too ashamed and too embarrassed to go home, I stayed in a shelter. I remember my first time going there. It's literally just like you see on tv. You can only be admitted during a certain time of the day, and women with children are first. So I knew my chances of getting in were low. Fortunately for me, there was this lady in line and she asked me why I was there. I told her I was homeless. I told her I had nowhere else to go, I was a college dropout, and I had quit my job so I got evicted from my apartment. She said, "Well they aren't going to let you in here by yourself, so just say you're my child." Gratefully, I said, "Okay." During my experience in the shelter, I got three-hots-and-a-cot. However, the rules and restrictions made me feel like an inmate. Yet, in my mind, it was better than going home feeling like a failure.

Left, Left, Left Right Left! Anybody who has ever been in the military knows exactly what this meant. It was during this lowest point of my 18 years of being on this earth that I met a man who I felt, at that time, was going to change my life for the better. "Thank you, Jesus! I dodged a bullet, things are looking better for me. I'm in the clear!" At least I thought I was. Hope came in the form of a tall black man with all these promises, and I believed him because I knew he had to be God-sent. I felt like my recruiter couldn't have come at a better time. He said, "Uncle Sam wants you!" And I believed! It was my way out! So, I said, "Let me just enlist and get the hell out of here!"

Once I passed all the required tests and exams, I decided it was time to go home. Feeling like I had redeemed myself, I was able to go home with my head somewhat held high. In my young mind, my pride and my college failure would not allow me to go home before I knew I had a plan. Feeling accomplished, I received my date to ship out for Bootcamp. I had a clear plan for the next phase of my life. Then the unexpected happened. My high school sweetheart came back to town and guess who wants to get married! Yes, he asked if I would marry him, and I said, "Yes". All the while, I was thinking to myself- "I'm damaged, used goods, naive, insecure, and a complete emotional mess!" Yet, I was still thrilled that he chose me.

I still felt I had my own career to pursue, so we both agreed that I would still go to the military with the under-standing that we would make our marriage work at all cost. Unfortunately, this was another short-lived dream. After several years of trying to make my career and marriage work, it was still a struggle. I requested to get stationed closer to my husband, especially after having our first son. My military career wasn't aligning up with what we needed as a family. So the sacrifice was made for me to give up my career while my husband stayed in and finished his. So when it was time to get out, I got out. I later figured out that the best job I had going for me was being a great mother of our now, two sons and a supportive military wife.

For over twenty years, I dedicated myself to these two roles. It was easy to give everyone all of me, except me. For years, I never felt like I put myself first. So, eventually, I became selfish and fed into the idea of not wanting to be the person everyone depended on, for so many years. I felt like this strain and emotional disconnect played the biggest part in the demise of my first marriage. I will never blame anyone for any decisions I made. My husband and I both agreed we had grown apart, and even though I tried fighting for my marriage after being the one who damaged it, like the song says- "Too Much, Too Little, Too Late."

For the first time in over twenty years, I was officially on my own again. What had I done now? Life had dealt me another heavy blow. "Somebody give me some air. I feel like I'm about to die!" I went through the worst depression. I thought I no longer wanted to live! Expressing these thoughts to my sister, literally got me a one-way ticket to the Psych Ward on the fifth floor of Camp Lejeune Naval Hospital. After four days of pacing the floors, sleeping on a metal bed with only a half-inch of mattress, standing in line in a paper gown waiting to take meds I knew I better hurry up and get myself together. This wasn't it! Embarrassed again that my new secret would get out, I told people I was in the hospital because of high blood pressure. After being released, I thought I had it together. *Fake It*

Until You Make It. Right? Not only was I dealing with a bitter divorce, but at this time, my oldest son was locked up in jail. I was the only one who would visit him, so I knew I had to get myself together. However, anybody who has ever dealt with severe depression understands it's not that easy to just snap out of it. I never had these kinds of emotions and hurt in my life, not even after the rape, so I was lost.

I now knew if I expressed the thoughts I was feeling it would land me back in the Psych Ward. So this time I was not telling anyone anything! I just wanted the pain to go away. I had tried being the best mom I could be, the best wife I knew how to be, the best organization leader I knew how to be. I tried treating people right, but it seemed as if the whole world was against me. My life as I knew it, was no more. "God I tried but I failed miserably." So I took a handful of the pills that I had received a few weeks prior, and I swallowed them all. I laid down for what I thought would be the last time, and yet, I still woke up the next morning. I thought to myself- "Damn, I can't get this right for nothing!" I was mad as hell and feeling awful. I never wanted to feel any pain like this, but I was. This time around I took myself to an in-town hospital instead of on-base because of fear of going back on the fifth floor.

When I arrived at the hospital, they immediately hooked me up to a few machines and ran several tests! They admitted me immediately! The doctor came in and said, "You are threatening a stroke." After further tests, it was determined that I had a light stroke, which was referred to as a TIA. I refused to tell the hospital what I had done. "Just treat me, stop this headache, and let me go home". Once I was released and finally made it back to my apartment. the place I thought I knew as my home was no more. I felt like an outcast. My church family turned their backs on me. People who I thought were my friends were really wolves in sheep's clothing. I told God, "I am mad at you! What are you keeping me here for? I can't take it anymore." After all of this, it was evident that I needed to head back to my home state of Georgia, and so that's what I did.

After being back home in Georgia for not even six weeks, I received a knock at the door informing me that my oldest son was killed in what was called a *"Home Invasion Gone Wrong."* I said to myself, *"I'm not going to make it this time. God, you failed me again and you are letting them drag my deceased son's name through the media. It is so much to deal with. I am so mad at you. I don't believe in you or your promises!"* My faith in God no longer existed. I cried out asking God- *"What did I do so bad that you are punishing me for the rest of my life. However, many days you see fit for me to be on this earth I'm supposed to do without my son, my first true love?"* And although I knew I still had my youngest son to raise, the depression crept back up on me again, but who could blame me. I lived a life of grief and torment. I thought about my oldest son all day. It was hard for me to decide to stay here and raise the one I had versus take my life and find the one I lost.

During the loss of my oldest son, my youngest son, Amari, and I were still living with my Mom. I owe my Mom all my love and dedication for supporting me during that difficult time. So after I finally caught enough wind to move around a little. My son, Amari, and I finally got our own little apartment which was just fitting for us. Those were the times when everything seemed like a fog. I was really trying now to take it slow because each day it was getting even harder to breathe. My new normal was not what I anticipated. I screamed and hollered every day for months waiting for my child to come through that door and tell me it was all a bad dream. And there were so many times I tried to hide it from Amari. However, when he came home from school, he quickly could tell what my day had been like. He would literally run into my room and try pulling me out of my closet, where he left me that morning. Sometimes having not moved all day; having not washed all day and having not eaten all day. Debating with myself on life and whether I still wanted to live. I expressed this to Amari and he told me, "*Momma, you all I got, we all we got. If no one else needs you, I d*o." It was at that moment I made the decision to live. I felt like I needed confirmation because my boys were my life, my reason, and even though half my reason was gone my other half was still here.

Life as I once knew it no longer exists, so many new things have altered me and shaped who I am today. Sometimes my anxiety still gets the best of me, although my therapist supplies me with the tools to help me control it. Since the passing of my son, I no longer desire to be around a lot of people anymore, and I'm okay with that. My son left me with this precious little girl who calls me *MeMe*. I love this child with all my heart. My boys are still my world, that will never change. I told myself I had my chance at marriage, and I had a good run at it. Little did I know what God had in store for me. After dating for over a year, I got married again! I'm now living in Charleston, South Carolina, and loving the area. Even after all the loss that I've endured and the disappointments in my life, I was allowed to love again. I still have my why-me-days, but for the first time in a long time, I feel as if I have a purpose and I don't think I'm excluded from life happening to me. I'm not the same person I was since losing my first love, and I embrace the change. I just feel like I've seen so much of the bottom that there is nowhere else for me to go other than to the top...The only difference is that now, I no longer hide my scars!

Love Notes:

Love Notes:

Author Anthony Taylor

Author Anthony Taylor

Mr. Anthony Taylor is a master communicator who has positively influenced the lives of thousands of individuals throughout the District of Columbia, Maryland, and Virginia Metropolitan Area over the last 25 years and he has only just begun. Mr. Taylor began his career in the field of law enforcement and later moved his talents to an arena where he could influence societal change with his dynamic voice. He has a history of equipping, engaging, and empowering young boys and girls of all ages.

Mr. Taylor is very knowledgeable and quite experienced with working with young people. He has worked as an assistant teacher, a youth counselor, a wrestling coach, a mentor for college students, and a life coach for at-risk youth. Mr. Taylor used each of these positions to speak into the lives of young people and help them understand what they are capable of. Working in this capacity has allowed him to build a powerful platform of inspiration, motivation, and education.

Mr. Taylor has held a number of different positions including a Youth Counselor, Assistant Teacher, Pretrial Service Officer, Community Supervision Officer (Probation/Parole Officer), and Federal Air Marshal. Mr. Taylor's experience in the area of Law Enforcement is comprised of 25 years as a protector of the community and four years defending the United States as a member of the United States Armed Forces. Even with the amount of time actively engaged in the field of law enforcement, Mr. Taylor continued to hone his skills and knowledge via training at the Federal Law Enforcement Training Center (FLETC) in Artesia, New Mexico. While Mr. Taylor spent a considerable amount of time participating in law enforcement activities, he still found time to become a certified personal trainer and spin instructor. Working in these different positions has taught Mr. Taylor the power of teamwork and how to share this powerful concept of unity without stripping these young people of their uniqueness. Mr. Taylor is certified in *Controlling Anger and Learning how to Manage it* (CALM).

In an effort to extend his reach and broaden his impact within the community, Mr. Taylor is the Founder and CEO of CME SPEAK LLC and CME SPEAK Foundation, which includes 'Motivate One – Inspire All' for the purpose of helping individuals, within the communities, to develop strong communication skills through motivational speaking, inspirational speaking, and team building. CME Speak has created a platform for Mr. Taylor and his personally selected dream team of speakers, to use their voices and life experiences to help young people navigate the minefields that occasionally accompany the teen years. Many of the lessons taught to these young people came by way of personal experience which is why Mr. Taylor and his dream team can teach with passion.

Mr. Taylor is a volunteer wrestling coach for the Laurel Maryland Boys and Girls Club. He has also served as a mentor and coach for at-risk youth within the Washington Metropolitan Area, which has allowed him to assist young men and women reach their full potential. Working in this capacity has allowed him to build a powerful platform of inspiration, motivation, and education. Mr. Taylor also helps participants step into a new position, which is an unheard of positive position, as a role model for communities at large.

Mr. Taylor is an active member and deeply involved with the Prince Hall Masons within the jurisdiction of Washington DC, where he is a Master Mason. Mr. Taylor is also a Prince Hall Shriners, an Auxiliary pf Ancient Egyptian Arabic Order Nobles Mystic Shrine (AEONMS) Washington DC, where he held the highest position as the Illustrious Potentate. While both of these organizations advocate strong relationships within their respective communities, each organization's passion is to serve the families within the community. These organizations are devoted to developing leaders; they are proponents of education, mentorship, and providing the kind of support that embodies Friendship, Morality, and Brotherly Love.

Coached to Win, Mentored in Love

My name is Anthony Taylor, and I am a transformational coach dedicated to helping people discover their magic. I am so passionate about coaching and mentoring because it not only changed my life, it *saved* my life. I would not be sharing my story if God had not placed people in my life who saw something inside of me, that I had no idea existed. My coaches and mentors loved me just because and it has been my life's mission to give back what they gave to me.

Each of us was gifted with a unique set of tools and abilities, which, for many, lie dormant awaiting activation. My life's journey, which includes phenomenal educational experiences, state-of-the-art training in a number of life-influencing fields of study, and the lessons I learned as a student of life, have positioned me to speak to the nation and the world. The reason I decided to dedicate my life to empowering the youth is because someone, with nothing to gain, showed me a different kind of love and spoke life into me when I was young and living on the edge. My journey could have gone either way, but their words, their time, and their *love* redirected my life.

The altered path that I took allowed me to participate in new learning experiences and empowered me to speak to as well as uplift diverse groups of people, which became second nature. Young people from the age of 12 to 24 interest me most. This group of young people will be picking up the baton and moving our nation forward. A considerable portion of my time and resources are reserved for young people who might be considered 'at risk'. I am so committed to this group because they are, who I was before love was spoken into my life.

I started an organization called CME SPEAK, which is not only committed to helping the leaders of tomorrow tap into their magic but this organization is also committed to sharing an agape type of love that will help sustain these young people when challenges arise. We assist this population, many of whom are on the verge of making decisions that could have a negative impact on their future and on the future of the community in which they live. Cultivating a talent-latent group of young people is not something that usually happens during a one-time encounter, which is why CME SPEAK is actually a mentoring organization as well. As the saying goes, '*kids do not care how much you know, until they know how much you care.*' This type of understanding takes time, but fortunately love is patient. With patience, we are able to see how different a person's life can be if they were to receive some assistance and support wrapped in true love. They learn that together, we can create a new way of living. This is a new life, filled with possibilities and promise.

You may be asking, what qualifies me to speak to this group? I have over 25 years of government service, but that is not what qualifies me. I have multiple certificates, degrees, and other accommodations, but that is not what qualifies me. I have received numerous awards for Military Veteran appreciation but that is not what qualifies me either. What qualifies me, is my desire to end suffering and bring hope to a population that far too many people are ready to write off or incarcerate.

While I am deeply immersed in teamwork and unity, at this point in my life, that is not how my story began. I came from a very small town and can say, from extremely humble beginnings as well. A formal education was not encouraged in my family. Work was promoted and once a child reached an age, when they were eligible for employment, they would get a job, which was critical to family survival. The importance of education was not promoted in my family nor in my community, therefore education was never embraced. Although there were men, in my family, they would not be considered role models or someone positive to emulate in any way. They did not have a clue about making their life better and they could not teach me what they did not know. Love, by the way, was a foreign concept in my household after my grandparents transitioned.

Although my living situation was less than ideal, it planted seeds in me for a better life that would take many years to blossom. I made a promise to myself that I would work hard, dream big, and put forth the effort necessary to make the promises I made to myself come true. I had no idea how I was going to do this, but I knew, I could do it. There is an old expression that says, *"when the student is ready, the teacher will appear."*

My memories of myself, during elementary school and even high school, were so far away from the man that I have become. As a child, I was so unsure of who I was and my purpose for life. I had so many questions about life and I didn't know anyone qualified to answer them for me. Many of the toughest battles, that I had at that time, took place between my ears and they were fought daily. Generational curses were in full effect and my life was following in the footsteps of so many that came before me. My life changed when I was asked by an assistant volunteer wrestling, Coach Mr. John Holliett, to join the junior high wrestling team. Coach Holliett instantaneously gave me a sense of self-worth, and a feeling of belonging; something that I had never felt before. Coach Holliett introduced me to trust, which is not something that I was exposed to in my household.

Through fellowship and training, Coach Holliett taught me the importance of setting goals and how they were the key to accomplishing anything I put my mind to. I instantaneously felt gratitude, resulting in a boost of self-esteem. Through our mentor/mentee relationship, I learned how to process shame, guilt, embarrassment, and a ton of other emotions that I had weighing on my shoulders. These were emotions that no one had ever taught me how to deal with. Coach Hollett played a vital role in my development as a man and he wrapped it up in the sport of wrestling. Indirectly, Coach Hollett taught me about the power of love and how it could alter the course of a person's life.

Coach Holliett provided a formal introduction to the Coaching team of Dan and Tommy Ternes. The Ternes brothers, who were the high school wrestling coaches, challenged me right away to think beyond my childhood limitations. The brothers always encouraged me to believe in my potential and *"God-Given Talent"*. I was challenged and provided opportunities that changed the course of my life. I was consistently reminded to practice hard, dream big, and believe things well beyond my neighborhood. The Ternes brothers provided activities, during and after the Wrestling Season, to ensure that my time and energy were put to good use. The Ternes brothers were very creative in keeping me on track and out of trouble. Activities were utilized to minimize opportunities to go astray. Activities included, but were not limited to; wrestling camps, tournaments, working high school concessions stands for local sporting events, visiting and helping with projects on the Ternes' farm, and daily self-improvement. The Ternes Brothers provided guidance and direction, something that was not provided at home. Their leadership, trust, and guidance gave me a sense that someone genuinely cared for my well-being.

After I graduated from high school, I entered the United States Army *'So I Could Be All I Could Be.'* This provided an opportunity for me to continue to learn and grow to the fullest extent possible. Entering the United States Military was an eye-opening experience for me. Instantaneously, structure, responsibility, and accountability became a part of my life. The new lifestyle, which meant following orders, was an eye-opening experience. The United States Army provided real-life situations inherent with an unlimited number of growth opportunities. Application of what I had been learning was required for my survival and I did it. I saw that I could set and achieve goals if I applied myself. While my life was definitely on a different trajectory, I still had a great deal of suppressed emotions that needed to be addressed. Because they had not surfaced properly and been dealt with in a satisfactory manner, I still made a lot of unhealthy choices. *More on that later.* Upon exiting the United States Military on November 28, 1988, this soldier was destined to pursue a college education.

In many instances, it felt like the family dysfunction that I worked so hard to overcome was on my heals, gaining ground quickly. I did not know how much my past and the habitual behaviors that I observed growing up would continue to impact me. After leaving the United States Army, I returned home and it seemed like dysfunction was waiting at the airport to greet me. Although my power of discernment would not have been considered refined at that time, I could see, "*I knew you would be back*" in the eyes of many of the people that I encountered. Spending time in that environment did not help my decision-making, and I began to fall into some potentially dangerous behavioral patterns. The journey to success may seem long, but the journey back to where you began is surprisingly short.

Just as I was on the verge of throwing away all of my potential, in steps love. The Ternes Brothers, my high school coaches, and mentors, moved me away from the negative environment, with its increasing influence on my life. I guess they knew that the negative elements that I grew up around would be too strong to overcome without a constant influx of positivity and love. So in the summer of 1989, my high school wrestling coach, Dan Ternes, sent me packing to a Junior College in Susanville, California. Upon arrival, I headed to the home of the Head Wrestling Coach. This is where my first introduction to Coach Dave Foster took place. Coach Foster was a man of many hats. Coach Dave Foster was the Mayor of Susanville, Professor at the Local Junior College, and the

Head Wrestling Coach. More importantly, he became my mentor and the father figure that I never had.

After arriving on campus, it was determined that I did not meet the criteria necessary to be admitted to college. What happened next is something that I was so unaccustomed to; people not abandoning you when challenges arose. Coach Foster, along with the school phycologist, Bernadette Chavez, created a plan of action that would put me on a track to become college eligible and the best collegiate wrestler. Coach Foster made arrangements with staff members, students, and other athletes to ensure that I attended classes and tutoring sessions. It seemed like eyes were always on me because if I missed a class or tutoring session without a legitimate reason, there was hell to pay!

Susanville, California was a place where I was broken, fixed, and prepared for success in life. Coach Foster was brutally honest in his dealings with me and spoke truth in a loving, but in-your-face manner. Coach Foster held me responsible for all of my actions, period. He would not tolerate excuses of any kind. Because I had to take responsibility for myself, I was forced out of my care-free attitude toward life, and I had to assume the mantle of leadership in my life. Coach Foster instilled a phrase in me that I can still hear in his voice to this day and that is, *"Failure is not an option."* As a result of Coach Dave Foster's, fair but firm approach, I received an Associates of Arts Degree in Administration of Justice from

Susanville Junior College and became the California Community College Wrestling Champion. As a result of my academics, *something I never thought I would say*, and wrestling prowess, I was recruited by Coach Jason Liles of Montana State University Northern, formerly known as Northern Montana College, which is located in one of the most picturesque places on earth Harve, Montana.

The coaches and mentors that I had, taught me to channel my desire for a better life into tangible actions. They taught me to use the fact that I was living in a two-bedroom home, with no indoor plumbing as a reason to push forward. They taught me to use the family dysfunction as the fuel to keep me pushing when my mind said I had done enough. They taught me to use the power of my mind to transform the extremely negative thoughts circulating in my mind into life-affirming thoughts. My coaches taught to destroy my preconceived physical and mental thresholds. I truly began to believe that I could do anything and from this posture, anything was possible.

As I continued on my success journey, I was introduced to coaches, mentors, and leaders who helped introduce *Antony Taylor* so the world could know the man hiding behind the façade of *I'm okay*, *family dysfunction*, and *pain*. These were difficult, but necessary introductions to the *real* me.

Lessons Learned:

1) **Embrace Success.** Your success may come from strange and unexpected places. Throughout my life, people with no biological connection to me showed me love and directed me towards the life path that was meant for me. Remain open, and great things will happen to you.

2) **Your Similar Story will Resonate.** Magic is meant to be shared. God has placed gifts inside of us that will have a positive impact on the lives of others if we are courageous enough to release them. Inside of you is the key to unlock the door of happiness for a group of people languishing in misery. Because our struggles mirror theirs, the relief they seek must come from someone who truly understands where they are coming from.

3) **Work for It.** The thought of hard work has derailed more dreams than the actual hard work itself. We are built for the **work** required to make our dreams a reality and to provide a positive touch for others along the way. Humanity was created to work together and together we can achieve more.

4) **Mentoring is love.** Be willing to share more than your talents and give your time. Reading your story is great but hearing how you overcame challenges, directly from you, is potentially life-changing. My mentors saved my life and your story will save the lives of many who will follow you. Don't be afraid to share your warts and the other icky parts of your story because it will resonate with someone and help transform their thinking and their life.

Love Notes:

Authors Bennie Harris

Author Bennie Harris

Bennie T. Harris lll was born and raised in the nation's capital of Washington DC, and still currently resides in the Washington Metropolitan area. Mr. Harris is happily married to Gerly Sapphire Harris and he has two awesome children, Dejeune and Domonick, and one amazing grandson Isacc.

Mr. Harris is currently employed by George Washington University where he has worked in a number of different capacities. Mr. Harris attended Howard University and Prince Georges County Community College. Mr. Harris is an avid reader, who is committed to learning and takes several courses a year, so that he can continue to grow. Mr. Harris believes in the Japanese principle of CANI, which stands for *constant and never-ending improvement*. Mr. Harris is also dedicated to passing along the knowledge and wisdom, that he acquires, to the youth and underserved populations. Mr. Harris believes that it is his job to improve and get better, in every area of his life, he can inspire others, from all walks of life, to do so as well.

Mr. Harris believes that there is greatness in everyone and he works hard to help others discover their magic. Mr. Harris is a master communicator and he is adept at sharing his voice and helping others discover theirs. Mr. Harris is a motivational speaker, writer, and editor. Mr. Harris has spoken for and made presentations at George Washington University, the Kiwanis Club of Washington DC, the National Congress of Black Women, The College for Kids, and incarcerated youths throughout the Washington Metropolitan area just to name a few. Mr. Harris has tutored preschool children and children in elementary as well. Mr. Harris is also a professor and administrator for the College for Kids. Mr. Harris understands the power of teamwork and group dynamics and teaches these principles to young people, church groups, and in the business as well.

Love Without Limits...

The vision, creation, and release of *Love Chronicles* could not have occurred at a more opportune time than now. The world in which we live is long overdue for a reset. Humanity has witnessed enough drama, division, and heartache recently, to last a lifetime, but change is at hand. The only force in existence that can take, our society and our world from where we are to where we want to go as a collective, is *Love.* Love can liberate minds, emancipate hearts, elevate thoughts, and heal bodies and relationships, while enhancing everything that it touches. Love may not always be easy to describe, but it can be seen in our eyes, heard in our words, felt in our touch, and experienced in our spirit. Love is a dynamic force that cannot be captured, nor should it be. Love is meant to be experienced by one and all.

Any action that is infused with love will have magical effects. When this transformational force connects with and begins to work through the dreams residing in the heart of an individual, a love without limits is born. Words communicated, either orally or in written form, have historically been one of the most effective conduits of love known to humanity. I've witnessed preachers, politicians, and other powerbrokers mesmerize and move people with their words. I've also witnessed individuals with something valuable to say, speak in smaller settings and influence those who are listing in an impactful way. When used in a positive manner, our words can have a life-changing impact on the entire world. In fact, America's Bishop, T.D. Jakes may have expressed it best when he said, 'more things have been changed through communication than with a gun'. And this is where my story begins. My dream, although I did not always acknowledge it, has been to educate, equip, and empower people with my words. I wanted to use my voice to encourage others to live their dreams through my books, trainings, speeches, and articles.

I remember a lot of noise in my childhood. People talked at one another quite a bit, but not necessarily with another, and as a result, a lot of things were lost in translation. Effective communication was not always employed in my household and my way of dealing with the noise was to stay to myself. I lived in my imagination, but I had yet to develop positive images of myself. While I had dreams of doing well, I did not actually see myself accomplishing what I dreamed of. Touching lives with my words was my dream, but in reality, I was extremely shy as a child. I lived out that old proverb that said; *"a child should be seen and not heard."* Although I am quite comfortable speaking to groups of any size, at this point in my life, I did not start out this way. In fact, if a review of my early childhood was conducted, there were no signs or evidence that the seeds of a competent communicator resided anywhere within me. Speaking up and out was not something that I felt comfortable doing at that time. What an interesting paradox, I was a speaker in the making, afraid to use my voice.

This worthy aspiration, this beautiful dream that I held secretly in my heart was almost choked out, in its infancy, before it ever had an opportunity to grow. In addition to being reluctant to speak up, I ran into a number of potential dream killers at an early age. These dream killers were not easy for the younger me to identify and they wore disguises that were pretty difficult for me to see through. The first potential dream-killer that I crossed paths with was a teacher who had a very imposing physical stature. She stood head and shoulders above almost everyone, female and male alike, at the elementary school that I attended. She came off as a caring instructor, but I am not so sure.

There was an incident that occurred, when I was in the fourth grade, that I can remember as if it just happened yesterday. After taking a standardized test, which we now know are not necessarily administered in a way that will draw out the very best from minority students, this teacher pulled me to the side to review my score. The words she used to describe my test scores and her thoughts on my ability will never be forgotten. She said, 'the test indicates that you are barely above average. Wow ~ without considering my family situation, my health, or what may have been taken place in my life at that time, this teacher made an assessment in an area where she was not qualified. This 'teacher' attempted to place the *"cuffs of limitation"* on me knowing they would be hard to break and they were.

I enjoyed school prior to our encounter, but on that day school lost some of its luster, some of its shine. I considered this teacher's words as gospel and never even mentioned it to my parents. I began to view my ability differently and that was the moment that my relationship with the educational system shifted. School just wasn't quite the same anymore. The desire to move the crowd with my words was still alive but I had no idea how it would manifest in my life. A few years later I had another encounter with a teacher, who must have been from the same dream-killing family. By this time, I was thirteen years old and my grades were in a free fall. Not only were my grades bad, but my self-identity was suffering as well and I lived it out in my behavior. I didn't think I was very smart and my results mirrored my thoughts.

The encounter with my seventh-grade teacher was just as traumatic as the fourth-grade incident. After excitingly turning in a paper, I moved on to the next assignment. I soon realized that my teacher was not nearly as excited about my work as I was. She went out of her way to let me know what she thought of my efforts and she did it in front of the entire class. She said, and I quote, *"Bennie, you can barely write your name."* Wow, these were not easy words for me to receive especially in light of my still hidden desire to speak to the world. This teacher's statement was made in front of all my classmates and it stung, but my pride would not allow me to show it. By now I was moving in the wrong direction and I was picking up speed.

Fast forward a few years and my grades suck and I am heading absolutely nowhere fast. My parents and other people who cared for me used a multiplicity of words, some good and some that were not, but nothing changed in my life. My life pivoted, however, as the result of a picture that went past my mind into my subconscious. I remembered what I'd been taught and began to understand me. It was my ninth-grade year and the bell rang indicating the beginning of class. I was late on this day which was not uncommon for me at that time. When I arrived at my English class for some unknown reason I paused for a second before entering. I took a moment to look into the class and what I saw changed my life. My classmates were out of control. They were talking loud, being disrespectful, throwing paper, and looked nothing like students. This was an everyday occurrence that I helped create, but could no longer participate in. In that moment, I dreamed of getting good grades, which was amazing because it had been years since I had envisioned anything positive for my life.

I know God is orderly and always on time, but my tardiness on this day, was by divine design. Arriving late to class was one of the greatest blessings of my life. In that moment, I learned a few keys to success that have helped me throughout my life. I learned the power in decisions and the power in changing your perspective. One of the things that I learned on that day was, decisions can be made quickly and effectively. Napoleon Hill, author of *Think and Grow Rich*, which remains one of the bestselling books in history, said that, *"all successful people made decisions very fast and changed them very slowly if and when they change them at all."* The decision I made, in that moment, to change my academic direction has paid huge dividends in my life and in the life of my family.

I also learned the importance of perspective. Looking at the way I was living from a different vantage point made all the difference in the world. For starters, I began to look at myself differently. I learned that not doing your best on an assignment or a test did not mean that I was not cable. It only meant that a new strategy was needed or perhaps more work in that area was required for improved results. Both of those solutions are within reach and they do not require the approval, assistance, or validation of anyone else. I also learned that, *"All things work together for the good of them that love God, to them who are called according to His purpose"* (Romans 8:28). That good might not be apparent at the first glance, but it is always there somewhere if we continue to search. That lesson was important because when I began speaking to juvenile offenders (walking in my dream), I could speak truth to their situation from my heart to theirs. I could tell them from my own history, letting them know that someone else's opinion, no matter what position or title they held, did not have to become a reality. When unwanted events take place in life, know that the occurrence represents an experience, a learning opportunity and not an insurmountable barrier to your dreams.

Now back to my story. When I entered the room that day, I sat down, looked straight ahead, and did every assignment given to me in excellence. My level of focus changed dramatically as well, as I no longer gave energy to anything that was outside of my academic pursuits. Within two weeks I was moved to a higher achieving class, and I never looked back academically. I also went from barely passing my classes to making the honor roll with consistency. This dramatic change in my academic performance had nothing to do with my cognitive ability, it occurred because I changed how I saw myself and fell in love with that person. As a result, my dream of communicating to the world was revived.

Our dreams are birthed through and out of love, although they are not always birthed into a loving environment. The teachers that I encountered early in my academic career could not see the power of communication in me and that's ok because it was my dream and not theirs. The world may fight for your rights as a citizen, but nobody is going to necessarily fight for the expression of the dream that resides in your heart. Along the pathway to success, there will be many people and moments that will help propel you forward, but your success ultimately depends on you and your willingness to put in the work. Success also requires that you hold onto a picture of success in your heart and mind no matter what is taking place in the world around you. Truth be told, your gifts and talents are uniquely packaged for this time in history and if you don't release them the entire planet will miss out on your magic. *"There is a vitality, a life force, an energy a quickening that is translated through you into actions, and because there is only one of you in all time, this expression is unique. And if you block it, it will never exist through any other medium and it will be lost,"* according to famed dancer Martha Graham, and I would agree.

If you are reading this, know that you are a unique expression of a Divinity, placed on earth at this time to help alter the course of history. Game-changing ability lies within your dreams and the gifts you've been given to help make your dreams become a reality. This may sound like revolutionary talk and I guess to a certain degree it is. Revolution means moving away from one social order in favor of a new one and that definitely describes the times in which we are living. According to Ralph Waldo Emerson, the famed essayist and philosopher, *"if there were any one point in time when one would desire to be born in - is it not the age of revolution, when the old and new stand side by side, when the glories of the old can be compensated by the rich possibilities of the new, that is a good time."* Know that there is a global reckoning occurring, a revolution of sorts taking place right now and your energy is needed for the victory. Each of us has a role to play and everyone's participation is required for success. And who knows, it may just be your unique expression of love flowing freely through your gifts and talents that changes the game forever.

Remember, you are a gift to this world no matter what has taken place in your life up until this point. You are a unique one-of-a-kind instrument of love. The love expressed through you and your gifts can change an ordinary time in history to a moment that will never be forgotten. When this powerful force is harnessed and truly embodied, all of humanity will feel, express, and experience love without limits. When living in this beautiful state, nothing is impossible. The great part about this divine space is, as success is generated, it will feed off of and create more success. As good health is experienced, it will feed off of and create increasing levels of good health. As prosperity is generated, it will feed off of and create greater levels of prosperity in your life. In this space, greater levels of achievement are within your grasp, ***seize the moment!***

My life and my story have demonstrated the unlimited power of love and a dream. When combined, they become a very attractive and unstoppable force. As you walk into your dream and share your gifts, the power of love working through you will radiate a light in you that will help usher people out of the bleachers and into the game of life. Remember, it is not a gift until you give it away and there has never been a better time for change than now.

Love Notes:

Author Cecilia Vandervall

Author Cecilia Vandervall

Cecilia A. Vandervall was born in San Pedro, California, and currently resides in Baltimore County Maryland. She is a veteran of the US Navy, a volunteer in the community where she resides, working with the youth and parents. She volunteers at State Homeless Shelters, and with Safe Streets. She shares her stories across many states to women and men who are struggling with the disease of addiction. She also is a foster parent. Cecilia believes that the transition from a negative lifestyle is achievable through hard work and self-determination. Her primary focus is to transition African American females from welfare to self-sufficiency.

Her educational background includes attending public schools around the world due to her father being in the Navy. These opportunities afforded her a solid educational foundation. She has a bachelor's degree in business mathematics from Loyola College, earned her first master's degree in Human Services at Lincoln University, followed by her second master's in Public Health from Capella University. Cecilia is currently a candidate for the Ph.D. in Behavior Sciences and referenced as "All but Dissertation" (ABD).

Cecilia currently is employed with The Department of Health and Human Services where she has focused on the trends of welfare and disparity for more than 26 years. Her biggest accomplishments in the field are watching others become productive members of society. However, her greatest achievements are granted from her two children, a son, and a daughter, who watched their mom overcome the evils in life and grow to be the greatest motivator through her challenges. She taught them that *the journey is yours, trust the process*. Cecilia currently has one new granddaughter and she enjoys every moment she spends with her new grandbaby, especially church and Facebook time.

Her hobbies include dancing, fishing, camping, and reading. Her favorite singer is Gladys Knight and she was inspired by the writings of Yolanda Vanzant. Cecilia is also affiliated with multiple organizations: Order of Eastern Stars, Golden Circle, Heroines of Jericho, The Cyrenes and The Shrine. She really enjoys being a clown with The Shrine, clowns turn tears into smiles.

In reading her chapter, she hopes that her hard-won experiences will enlighten those who may have made the wrong turn on the path, that at any time they too, can find a new way of life. Cecilia believes that lost dreams are awakened and no mountain is too high to climb. She no longer says, "I'm trying," now she says, "I'm doing this with confidence and faith. God has not brought me this far to let me down now." As she unfolds her passages of hope, combines the horrors of beauty and pain, she encourages one to learn to forgive themselves and continue the journey. She never really finds that real love outside of herself and believes her passion to fulfill the emptiness and to hide all the hurts will heal only with time. Cecilia remembers the words from her grandmother, "But those who hope in the Lord shall renew their strength. Isaiah 40:31. Child, you are never alone!"

Never Alone

I still cry over all that happened in my life. The day everything changed. I call it life. All that counts is what you have done within the spaces, with the time, and with yourself. Nobody ever looks back and pushes pause, so that you can get yourself together. Stuff happens, and life goes on, with or without you. It's like my life has always been lived before the crisis and after the devastation. The hardest part is understanding my feelings along the way. What I do, have done, and will do, become my memories. The good, the bad, and the indifferent. This is my story and as it unfolds, keep an open mind because my journey is filled with loneliness, agony, and pain.

The truth of the matter is that I am scared, depressed, and all alone. Many people would describe me as outgoing; a loud talker, and the life of the party. As it turns out, all that is true but here's why....

We lived in California. I grew up with health issues; my mother had to give me constant care. I suffered severely from eczema and asthma. I was the first child of three. The oldest girl. The smart one with a big mouth. As I developed and grew up, I became rebellious toward my mother's rules. This all stemmed from watching my mother and biological father fight. I became jealous and resentful when my mother moved on to a better love. I thought she had forgotten me. I wasn't as needy once my skin cleared, but I still needed her. *"What about me? I'm here by myself and need you to continue caring for me; loving me and talking to me."* Therefore, I cried all the time, not knowing how to suppress these feelings. I remember one time my mother took an overdose of sleeping pills. I thought to myself, *"Oh my God, she is trying to leave without me!"* After my mother escaped from my father, she was back to giving me and my sister all her attention. My father had been so mean to her and to me. I was finally happy and so was my mother. As a child, I did not realize she now had full responsibility for us, and we had to go to *"real"* school. Oh well, at least the fights were over. We were not alone, we had my grandmother, Big Sister, and a host of cousins, aunts, and uncles.

As I grew up, I noticed that I was of a darker complexion than my sister. She was light-skinned. In my eyes she was beautiful, and I was ugly. In the 70s, being of a lighter complexion meant something. I still don't get it, but anyway, to compensate, I strived to be smarter. Only because I had nothing else going for me. I couldn't sing, dance or fight. My sister could do all that. Everyone liked those abilities and praised the children who could do those things. I was just smart, so I began to isolate myself early in life. I had to find some people to like me for what I could do. My mother found comfort in romance novels and soap operas. Well, I was in school when the soap operas came on tv, so I would steal her novels in search of that same joy she experienced.

Wow, the knight in shining armor, he was going to ride up in the back yard under my window. I was going to jump on the back of his horse, and he was going to take me to love and happiness. This went on for most of my junior high school days. My stepfather brought a motorcycle, so off he and my mother went, *partying* all weekend, every weekend. They would have guests over all the time. Family and friends and motorcycles! The grown-ups would drink and cuss. Most of the women were very pretty, and some were my complexion. They had things. The men liked them. I wanted to be like them. So I would always ask to help clean up when they left. Only to get some of the leftover drinks in the cups and cigarette butts. I waited for my parents to leave home and I would emulate all the activities of the grown-ups. Needless to say, by age 15, I was an undercover alcoholic.

I did not realize that was what I was becoming. Through the alcohol, I found love, and as long as I was feeling outside of myself, I did not care about any rules, my mother, or anything else. I was often depressed and lonely. I needed something to help me cope with my feelings. I was smart by day and drunk by night. Between reading romance novels and listening to sad music, I still cried. I was still alone; this was no longer enough. Soon, I found myself with people and in places, seeking to fill the void; to ease the feeling of being alone. It did not matter if it was dangerous, I drank my courage and it took me to all the wrong places.

This dark journey took me down many lows and this is where I met my first husband. Forgetting my dreams, forgetting college and that I had just come home from the Navy that Sunday and in three days I was at City Hall saying- "*I do*". It soon became clear that my husband had no desire to be anything other than a thief, and that was all I wanted because we got drunk and fought like cats and dogs. Once the euphoria wore off, I couldn't figure out how to leave or who to turn to. Frustrated, I began to drink with his uncle and found my new improved love. He worked for the railroad and loved my young body. He was my everything because he gave me things and money and moved me into a nice apartment *without* the husband. Well, the husband went to jail in Houston and that was better for me. The fights had stopped. It was just me and the uncle. Until he told me that his wife knew he was seeing me and had threatened him. I wasn't worried because I knew the arrangement wouldn't last, and I had stashed the money they told me to send to my husband in jail for my later days. I told you I was smart. Next….

I started to work at the chicken store during the day and bartended in the Bunny Club at night. Both places the uncle introduced me to. I began to date high-class professionals and moved to the penthouse. I had arrived. All the girls, light-skinned and dark, looked up to me. They all admired me. They showed me how to treat the game, and yes, there were rules to the game. Nothing like my mother's rules; these rules were new to me. I was a willing participant. I learned to dance enough to satisfy the male customers and even started a Corvette Club. I did not have a Corvette; I didn't even own a car. Yet, we had meetings, rules, and raced. I was on top. The men were now supporting my ideas because I was keeping their ego boosted. This is where I learned the lesson *"one hand washes the other,"* and on the flip side I learned, *"don't bite the hand that feeds you"*. I learned the lessons the hard way. Those rules get me every time. The hurricane destroyed that moment in time. I should have been happy about that, but instead, my world crumbled. All out of games and tricks on the path of destruction, once again I found myself alone and scared. I needed a drink so that I could think stuff through. In the streets of Houston, I sought out bars, alleys, and sometimes resorted to working the streets. Beep Beep…

He drove up in a car longer than a house, stuck his hand out the window, and asked, *"What's a girl like you doing in a place like this?"* I instantly lied and said, *"I ran out of gas and am trying to get home."* He opened the door. I thought I had found the one for me. He was tall, tall, tall. He smelled good and Lord, his clothes were expensive. My heart raced. This felt different. It was like love at first sight. I had to put back on my educated hat, I had to go back to my old way of speaking. He was very intelligent and studious; we had great conversations. After a long night of talking, I never left his side. He was everything. I went back to nursing at the hospital, which started as a lie. I had to up my game, he was a professional ballplayer. Living the good life, I forgot about the husband in jail, the bunny clubs, and everything else, even home. I devoted all my time and energy into making him happy. The people, places, and things kept me happy. He was popular, so that made me popular. Everybody in his circle loved me. I showed them no different, I wanted to stay, and the competition was thick. I would do anything to keep him. Basically, I did not need to do anything but be pretty all the time, even when I slept. After about five years, around the time of the changing of his contract, he began to change. I noticed it, but I dared to say anything. I wanted him to be proud of me, so I saved my money and brought a Grand Marquis. Shiny blue, rims and all. He became angry and started to fuss and fight. He left and stayed gone for many days. When he got back, he locked himself in the bathroom and would not open the door. When he finally came out, he asked for my keys. After being gone for several days, he came back to fight with me. I grabbed my keys and went off to work. It was Martin Luther King's birthday, so I had my headlights on all day. When I came out from work, my car would not start so I went into the trunk to get the cables and found drug paraphernalia. I spoke to him about it, and we fought until he threw me out naked. All I could do was cry. *"My love has beaten me and is on drugs! I needed a drink to get through this"* Here I am again, all alone, just me with nowhere to go.

Somehow, someway I lost myself in addiction on the streets of Houston, Texas. All the fame and glory were gone. The rules of the streets had changed just that fast. I was so alone, but if I stayed drunk something would happen… and it did. At my lowest point, I was beaten, raped, and left for dead. I couldn't report it because I had a problem and would go to jail. I was so tired of all of it but did not know how to stop and stay stopped. It wasn't until this guy came on the cut (in the alley) and uttered those same words,*"Why is a girl like you out here?"* I started to cry. He gave me the best advice, he said, *"If you get arrested, tell the judge you got a problem, and he will send you to treatment."* Without hesitation, I was off seeking a lock-up. It happened and when I was being processed in, I was told that I was pregnant. I will leave that right there for now. The judge did exactly what the guy said. I spent 90 days in a treatment facility and was released to a mission for the birth of my son. He was born healthy and sober. He was the answer to all my loneliness. I had this child who needed me, and I had made a mess of everything. All I knew to do was to call the very person I ran away from, my mother. My son and I arrived in Baltimore to open arms, hugs, and tears. It was different but good to be home. They all had no idea of my path. They all did not know how I missed my old life. I had been sober for over nine months, and I needed help. How do I tell my folks I have a problem? Somehow my stepfather knew something was wrong. So the next day he told me about these people who were always hugging and that he thought they could give me support. He took me and my son to my first meeting. It was all that he had described. They were in there saying things like- *"Don't leave five minutes before the miracle. Keep coming back."* And my favorite, *"YOU ARE NOT ALONE. "*

They shared their experiences as if they were all with me all along. I would sit, listen, and cry. I could relate to the pain. It was suggested that I get a sponsor to guide me through the process and so I did. Later, I got a temporary job with the agency where I work today as a supervisor. I met the man of men. He was all I could ever want. He made me laugh, we talked, and we shared the same interest. He was strong in recovery, and I knew he was more than enough for me. He was my friend, my world, and most of all, my love. In those 20 plus years, we had a baby together and got married. The perfect love, me, and him against all odds, raising our children, attending meetings, and working. In the meantime, something happened. I felt it, I couldn't describe it, but something was different. We went from laughing to criticism, accusations, and back to the tears. A stranger in my midst and I feel alone. Neither one of us wanted to be the first to say goodbye. All by myself and scared. I did not need a mind or mood alternating chemical to cope this time. I have the tools to cope. I live the program to save my life from the chains of self-destruction. Others have shared this experience and I stashed it for later. I needed a sponsor with the ammunition to keep me on the path. My sponsor and I talked and I cried through the process. I was lonely and I was sad. Each day brought on another feeling I never challenged. But I was never alone.

This way of life is not easy. I work on myself with the help of my sponsor. I had to learn to love myself and be by myself. Acceptance and Humility. After all, I have endured, now the rules and lessons are coming together. Everything my mother taught me has come to pass. I can look back on my life and know what I don't need to do and how to make better choices. Everything that looks good isn't good and always do the right thing for the right reasons. God sent me several angels on my journey and I learned from each experience. I have forgiven myself for all my wrongs over the years. I am no longer that clueless woman, searching for love in all the wrong places. I found it within. I am smart, I am beautiful and I am not alone.

Love Notes:

Love Notes:

Authors Darius & Sonia Lowery Scott

Authors Darius & Sonia Lowery Scott

Sonia Sheree Lowery-Scott was born in Sumter, South Carolina, and Darius Jermaine Scott is a native of Newark, New Jersey who was raised in Sumter, South Carolina. They currently reside in the Palmetto State known as South Carolina, in the city of Columbia. They enjoy spending time with family, friends and celebrating themselves as a couple. Darius and Sonia are high school graduates of Sumter High School, class of 1990. They have been together for a total of 37 years and married for 27 years. Darius & Sonia share the blessing of one son, Darius Jaikari, and one daughter, Jordyn Amiyah.

Darius served 26 years of service in The United States Army with great honor. He is now a proud army veteran who is committed to making a difference. Sonia has given over 24 years of dedicated service to the United States Department of Defense. This couple's passion is to help others be better today than yesterday. They work to inspire others to walk in faith and cherish each day as a gift. Darius and Sonia belong to several charitable organizations that include masonic affiliations. Sonia is also a member of Delta Sigma Theta Sorority, Inc. They have learned, in this season, that it is better to be obedient to God than trying to please others with their expectations of you.

MAKING IT LAST FOREVER

"To everything there is a season, and time to every purpose under heaven."
Ecclesiastes.3:1
"A Warm Smile is the Universal Language of Kindness."

We had some of our best days on the elementary playground. Darius would be playing basketball, and I would be in the back playing. Without parental permission, and contrary to elementary school etiquette, I had a boyfriend, and he was a friend of Darius. Darius' girlfriend was a friend of mine. It just so happened that our dates were brother and sister. *As the World Turns* in elementary school, Darius and I ended up dating, without my father knowing. Now you know, we only had *One Life to Live*, so we would break up to make up. Daily, Darius and I spoke by phone, sometimes just listening to the other breathe. Darius would use his cassette player and share all the songs by the artist, Keith Sweat.

Our favorite song was *"Make It Last Forever."* Now you have to understand the background. Darius relocated from New Jersey to South Carolina. My summer vacations included a trip to New Jersey and Ohio to see family members. In later years, Darius and I shared our summers in Jersey. Those were the *Days of Our Lives* from elementary to my freshman year in college and *Darius'* basic training in the army.

Now, there I was at our family's traditional college, entering to learn, departing to serve. My boyfriend was in basic training in the army. We wrote consistently and talked often, but I guess not enough. One young man from high school asked me for a date. I said, *"No, I am dating Darius."* He replied, *"How can you be when another girl is dating him?"* I questioned him, asking the five "W's". He gave me all the information I needed. I contacted this young lady, and we discussed the situation. Darius admitted to the relationship with the other girl, and I called our relationship off.

Just like any young, adolescent girl, I had imagined the perfect wedding. There were notes, clippings, pictures, and outdated wedding programs all archived. So, I began planning this elaborate celebration with all the bells and whistles, not sparing any pockets; I was ready. My family was fully involved. His family was on board. The church was reserved and the pianist was ready to play. The saxophonist was practicing his tunes, and the bridal gown and rings were purchased. Who knew in ninety days the groom would change?

As I rode with my husband-to-be, I caught a glimpse of *him*. I murmured his name before I knew it. Off in the distance, I heard my fiancé say, "What did you say?" Without as much as a blink of an eye, I kept staring, waiting for the license plate to go by. I said his name, "*Darius,*" uncertain as to why, but I dared not go any further with my thoughts. It was my fiancé's birthday. Later that evening, it was raining extremely hard, and it was cold in South Carolina. As I drove into my neighborhood, I could barely see through the windshield. Suddenly, I saw the same car, his car in our dead-end circle. There was only one way in and one way out. You knew everyone and their vehicles in the neighborhood. Why was he here? As a matter of fact, why was he even in my area? I wasn't looking to see my past coming into my present. Before he could turn into our gate, I stopped him!

As the cold raindrops beat against my face, I used a low tone voice and said, "*What are you doing here?*" Darius, without any hesitation, stated, "*I came to see you.*" I replied, "*Then follow me to my grandparents' home.*" Him being the perfect gentleman, obliged my request. For some reason, I don't recall any more rain; it went away.

Darius sported this grin on his face indicating- "*I got her!*" He was dressed nice and smelling real good. Ummm, umm, good! I then asked, "*What are you doing here?*" I asked with a stellar voice, in a tone that said- "*I am not interested, just curious.*" His cool reply was, "*I am on leave and was in the area.*" (No you weren't! I live on a dead-end street!) "*I just wanted to know if you wanted to go to the movies*", he said. Without thinking clearly, I said, "*Sure*", in my bold voice. In my mind, I asked myself, "*What are you doing?*" Go figure, the movie Darius selected was, "*True Lies.*" Now listen closely because this soldier had a road map but no compass. He leaned over during the film and said, "*Who are we fooling? Let's get married. My grandmother told me you've postponed and called that wedding off at least three times. She showed me the newspaper clippings of your accomplishments, and she and I are proud of you.*" I kindly replied, "Darius, I am engaged already." He said, "*Sheree, we were meant to be together.*" So, then I asked, "Are you dating someone?" "Yes, but she is married." Before I knew it, I said, "*Say what?*" Darius' response was, "*We can let both of them go, yours and mine.*" After some extensive conversation and us barely watching the movie, we kissed. Then Darius came back with, "*I am on orders to go to Hawaii, and I don't want to leave without you. We must be married for you to be on my orders.*" After the movie ended, we returned to my grandparent's home. Things were in an uproar; my grandmother called me into her room. She said to me, "*Sheree that other boy you promised to marry has been here looking for you.*" I humbly said, "*Okay, grandma.*" She went on to say, "I told him you went to the movies with that other boy." In my mind, I was saying, "*Really grandma, you dimed me out?*" Instead, I replied with, "*Yes, ma'am.*" Returning to the living room, I explained to Darius, "*My fiancé was here. He is looking for me, and he will indeed be returning.*"

My fiancé did indeed return, but to my surprise, so did my other family members. So, I did the Southern Belle thing. I did introductions. My family member instructed both gentlemen to go to their homes, and said, "*Sheree will call one of you tomorrow.*"

Only my fiancé couldn't wait for the call; the hour drive home must have gotten the best of him. He called me back and said, *"What was that?"* Without waiting for my response, he went on to say, *"I want all of my belongings, including the ring."* Then, without any anger or hesitation, I asked, *"Would you like me to mail it or bring it?"*

For the next few weeks, we were on a roller coaster. Darius' mother returned to New Jersey and at the airport, she told us, *"Don't rush into anything. Take your time."* After twenty-plus years, my mother retired from her position. All the family came from far and near to celebrate her retirement. Darius, stationed in Georgia, returned to base. We talked multiple times a day. He was not away from me for long, and he returned with a ring and a special request. I remember that it was indeed a beautiful Sunday, and we were just returning from our worship service. My father sat in his wheelchair with a toothpick in his mouth. My mother moved around the kitchen, as usual, completing the final touches for dinner. Darius asked my parents if he could talk to them, so my mom sat down. He said, with a confident voice, *"I would like to ask for Sheree's hand in marriage."* My mother said, *"What? She was just engaged to be married to someone else."* Darius spoke gently and said, *"It's like a bird. If you set it free and it comes back to you, it was meant to be."* Mommie said, "I am done with it". Then she utilized her phone tree to tell all the family members. When we arrived at Darius' grandmother's home, she was already aware of everything. She had seen the ring and knew just what Darius' actions were going to be. She politely told Darius, *"Remove the ring from her finger and do it the right way."* Darius did as told and went on bended knee and again asked me to marry him.

Have you ever heard your mother say there will be days like this? Well, first of all, Darius and I planned to go to the Justice of the Peace. Darius was on a field training exercise, and I was in school. Our funds were minimal, and we had several barriers to overcome. So we thought the ceremony should be something small and simple. My grandmother had already informed my mother that we couldn't go to the church. She explained her reason, "My granddaughter was supposed to marry someone *else* at that church." My mother agreed, and said, *"We are just going to have to do it at the house. I can't let her go to the courthouse."* Our marriage ceremony went from the courthouse to the church, to my parents' home, to my aunt's sun porch in a matter of days! We didn't think of creating a wedding party. However, my family member developed her own plan. She eagerly requested that Darius select a best man, and told me she would serve as my matron of honor. The dress and veil were already available. My family hired a florist, a photographer, a pianist, and ushers. We had an entire wedding in a matter of two weeks!

Our honeymoon went from plans for a trip to the beach to preparing for my new husband's deployment in the desert. After the wedding, I immediately changed out of my white gown into a black pants suit and immediately returned to base for Darius to be deployed. While Darius was on deployment status, I was making a house into a home. I completed college and worked purchasing furniture and more. Thanking and praising God, encouraged through numerous care packages, Darius finally returned home safely!

The Marriage: Communication was one of our biggest challenges. Darius being an introvert and me being an extrovert, complemented, but also hindered our relationship.

As the baby girl of my family, I was raised in a two-parent household with multiple challenges. My siblings were at least 10-13 years senior to me. I was spoiled, sheltered, set in my ways, with my own schedule. Darius, on the other hand, was raised by a single mother and later by a grandmother and extended family, with no father figure.

As a result, we had two very different child-rearing styles. This was definitely a challenge in our marriage. There were times we didn't know how to communicate effectively. As we would relocate to our various duty stations, we would find a new church to join. We continued to serve in multiple auxiliaries as we were taught. We were seeking spiritual guidance to work on building a healthy relationship. We met with numerous counselors, chaplains, and attended lots of marriage retreats. We were practicing church, but we were not evenly yoked. Our spiritual connection was all over the place, and our lifestyle included the nightclub.

I even asked one minister, *"What's wrong with me going to the club?"* The pastor informed me, *"If you can go into the club and come out the same way you went in, you will be fine."* I discovered in later years what that meant. Your relationship with God has to be strong enough to enable you to withstand temptation.

We both enjoyed family, friends, music, watching movies, attending church, but something was missing. Dancing to the old school blues music was my thang, but Darius enjoyed the booming system with hip hop and R&B; we were disconnected. So the outlet I used was to go, dance, listen to good music, and share in adult beverages at the club.

Darius didn't dance, or drink, and he didn't care too much about socializing; he was an introvert. I was the opposite; I had never met a stranger. I could strike up a conversation with anyone about anything; I was a true extrovert. The issue was that the attention I received at the nightclub felt good. I would clean, cook, and then dress to impress when I attended all the parties without my spouse. Yes, that invited attention I enjoyed, and it created the opportunity for me to step outside of my marriage covenant.

It was not long after, that Darius found attention elsewhere, too. We both were in a marriage but were no longer committed to our vows or each other. We had permitted extramarital affairs to consume our minds and time. After numerous conversations, plans, and actions about separation and possibly divorce, we decided to try communicating again. During angry disagreements, we found neither of us was listening to the other. Instead, we were just talking *at* each other, and not *to* each other.

After a brief separation, Darius called to wish me a Happy Anniversary. I questioned him and said, *"What's so happy about it?"* On that anniversary, I got no flowers and no gifts, but neither did Darius. On one visit, Darius asked, *"Can we talk?"* In one night, we laughed, cried, shared, communicated, and we hugged. Then, he asked, *"Did you cook?"* I said, *"Absolutely."* Then adding with a smirk, *"We eat well every day."* After a home-cooked meal, he said, "Do you mind if I just stay the night here?" I immediately said, *"No, sir, you can't."* He asked, *"Are you serious? "Are you kidding me?"* I said, *"Absolutely not."* I spoke with that bold, cocky attitude, *"But call me and let me know you made it in safely."* How many of you know I was waiting for the phone to ring? Sometimes you have to give up a U for the US. When the phone rang, I answered and said, *"Hello, is it me you're looking for?"* Paying tribute that to Lionel Richie. He said, *"Yes"* after a short conversation. The rest of the evening was fascinating! Needless to say, the song we woke up to was, *"As We Lay."* Our family was back together again.

In order to rekindle the flame and keep it ignited, we willingly forgave each other for the affairs. During our Come-to-Jesus meeting that we still have often, we share the good, bad and ugly. We have learned in this season it is better to communicate than to allow others to believe they have victory over us. We have engaged in the process of- *"ye with no sin cast the first stone."* (John 8:7) People will hold you hostage, thinking they have the upper hand. They will share memories, stories of how you used to be instead of where you are now. It is easier for them to keep you in an awful situation. They refuse to believe God loves you with all your faults. God has the power to transform and renew!

"To everything, there is a season, and time to every purpose under heaven." (Ecclesiates.3:1) *"A Warm Smile is the Universal Language of Kindness.*

Love Notes:

Love Notes:

Author Dr. Contress Michelle Braxton

Author Dr. Contress Michelle Braxton

The Honorable Apostle Dr. Contress Michelle Braxton is a native of New York City, New York; she currently resides in the Washington Metropolitan area. She is the oldest of eight children; she has over 30 nieces and nephews and is the proud Godmother of at least 13+ godchildren-7 boys and 6 girls and counting. She is a grandmother to three handsome boys and one beautiful girl. She has served as a foster care parent to four teenagers. Dr. Braxton truly has a heart and love for children. Dr. Braxton acknowledged Jesus Christ as her personal Lord and Savior at an early age.

Dr. Braxton graduated high school in 1988, started her career in the Food and Drug Administration (FDA) in 1989, and is still working for the government today as a Consumer Safety Officer. While furthering her education for her job, Dr. Braxton's career path began to shift. She was very active in the Church, earning her Associate of Arts degree in ministry, Bachelor's, Master's, and Doctorate Degrees in Religious Education, all at the NHL Institute where she currently serves as an Associate Professor. She earned her Doctorate in Divinity, Ph.D. in Philosophy of Religious Studies, and her Doctorate of Humane Letters (honoris causa) at Breakthrough Bible College (BBC). She is Pastor and Founder of her own Church-God's Divine Ministries International House of Refuge (formerly God's Divine Ministry(ies), Inc.), an Ordained/licensed Chaplain, a Christian Solo Artist, and a member of Delta Psi Epsilon Christian Sorority. One of her favorite scriptures is found in the book of 2 Timothy 2:15 *"Study to shew thyself approved unto God, a workman that needeth not to be ashamed, rightly dividing the word of truth."*

Dr. Braxton has served and continues to serve her community in many different capacities. She is a lifetime/gold plus member of Blacks In Government (BIG) and a graduate of the Darlene Young Leadership Academy (DYLA) Executive Leadership program. She's held several prominent positions in this organization; specifically, National Executive Vice President, President of founding Chapter

Parklawn, and Regional Representative. She also serves as a member of the National Congress of Black Women Disability Committee. Dr. Braxton is a coordinator for different events (i.e., funerals, weddings, conferences, etc.) and she loves to sing, dance, teach, present, bowl, travel, and attend family gatherings. She is a woman who doesn't serve to be seen but rather to be seen serving. May her chapter uplift, inspire, motivate, and persuade you to want to continue your life's journey no matter what life brings your way.

Contact Information Website:
Email: gdmhr8@gmail.com or pasdrb69@gmail.com
LinkedIn:
https://www.linkedin.com/contress-braxton-977a5a126
Facebook:
https://www.facebook.com/contress.braxton
Instagram:
@contressbraxton7
Twitter:
@contressbraxto1

THE AGE OF 19?

Alcohol, drugs, mental, physical, verbal, and sexual abuse- by When would it end? Can I become more than my environment? Who and what would I become?

Growing up as the oldest child wasn't easy. Couldn't do a lot of kid things- cooking, cleaning, and babysitting were my fun time activities. My friends were limited, but I had them, so I didn't complain. Growing up on welfare was a saving grace, but it was not a happy and enjoyable way to live. Being teased, talked about, and called names never made it easy. Every day was a chore; to have to get up and go to school in the morning knowing that I had to come home and start all over again. The hardest part was watching someone you love being abused and mistreated to the point of almost losing their life. What child could grow up and be okay in this environment? It wasn't okay. Not only was my mother being physically abused, but her two oldest boys were having to encounter some of the same abuse. I on the other hand dealt with abuse that challenged my mental wellbeing. Accusations that caused me to leave home at the age of 19, with no true understanding of what was out there waiting for me. During all that was happening in the household, a God I did not know was making provisions for me.

My dad left home when I was six or eight years of age, I cannot remember. I was molested at a young age. Again, the memories are dim and the exact age is not clear. At age 12, I was accused of sleeping with my mom's man because I was crying and didn't like to see people be physically abused. I had low self-esteem to the point where I attempted to commit suicide at the age of 13. I didn't go through with it because my mom told me I wouldn't make it into heaven. School became a hard task because my nights were longer. After school, while others went out to play, 95% of the time I was babysitting, cooking, cleaning, and being made to take care of other things that an adult should handle. My mom's health was not the best, so I had to help her as well. Washing walls was a whole different chore and a white glove test meant a redo and late night. I didn't really have anyone to share my issues with at home, so I ran my mouth at school to those who said they were my friends, but in truth, couldn't care less about me. So much for keeping family secrets. For me it was a release, for others, it was just wrong. This began late-night walks and strolls on long highways and through wooded areas talking to a God I did not know. I knew He existed, but I did not know Him.

Was this my whole life? Was this all that existed for me? Who knew that coming home one late night and being accused of hurting my mom would change my life at 19? So, with all the drama and abuse, did I have any fun, any dreams, or any purpose in what I called a sad life. Well, I did. Just about every summer I would go home to New York and hang out with my grandparents, aunts, and uncles; I would look for my dad hoping to talk with him and get to know him. I remember dreaming when I was eight years old of having a family: a husband, at least two kids, and a house. I shared it when I got older, and they laughed and would say, *"Something is wrong with you. It's eight of you all, and you never really have time to hang out and do teenage things. Why would you want kids?"* Funny thing- I went from two kids to wanting four. I wanted to be a Solid Gold dancer, a singer, and an actress. In high school, I was in a couple of plays, one that earned me an A in English, *The WIZ*. I played Evilene and was good at it. I felt a sense of pride in that role because it represented to me, at that time, who I thought I was going to become. A controlling, evil, want-to-be witch. I was called so many other names it was befitting. But I had fun. I enjoyed that time because it was about me. My family showed up in great numbers to see me in that play. Then something happened.

I started hanging out with friends when I could. I learned to drink malt liquors, peach schnapps, Miller Lights, and Coronas with a lime, to name a few. Trying to become an alcoholic. My two older brothers left home and went to live with family in New York. I began clubbing and becoming promiscuous and a tease. I was looking for love from whoever and wherever I was big and bad enough to get it. I could not smoke or get high off weed and other drugs, so I just hung around those that did. Doors started opening, both good and bad. How could that be, you might ask? Well, the first thing that happened was I dated a drug dealer, who is currently serving three life sentences for murder. I was date-raped by another guy I was dating. His brother tried to help me the first time. I didn't report it because I told myself that I deserved it. If I can be a little forward, I was a virgin, and back in those days, I was told that he was just- *busting my cherry*.

After ending the relationship, a year later I was raped by the *same* guy. How on earth could that happen? Well, his mother was dying, and she wanted to see me. I asked if he was there and they said, "*No*." So, I went by to see his mother; he wasn't there. She asked me to go upstairs in the house and change some music for her, so I did. Before I could turn around to come back downstairs, there he was. I was fighting for my life. He took what he wanted and left me there. When I got myself together, I left and never looked back. I couldn't even say goodbye to his mother. My life changed again. I got a grip, I tried counseling with a therapist, but couldn't continue, and didn't care. I began to spiral but did not know it. Dating became a walk around the block. I had a few serious relationships, but they didn't last long. You see, I was the stuff, and I could get who and what I wanted when I wanted it. However good I thought it felt, I was never satisfied. It wasn't enough. I was raped several times after my first time. They weren't enough. Could it get any better than this I thought to myself? In the meantime, my life in the church began to pick up.

Between the rapes, physical abuse, and drinking, I graduated high school but the thought of college was out of the question. My life didn't allow it, I thought. I went to business college and trade schools. After finishing them, I took the civil service test twice and I got a job. The blessing in this was how I got the job. We did not have a phone during that time, so my neighbor up the street allowed me to use their number. A week had gone by and I happened to go and visit my neighbor. I was told that I had received a call from the Food and Drug Administration (FDA). It had been about a week since the call came in. I just knew I wasn't going to get an interview because of the timeframe. I called the number and was given an interview! Went on the interview with red hair and a royal blue dress with dark blue dots. A week later I received a call stating that I had the job and would start on September 10, 1989. I have been working for the FDA ever since. As soon as that happened, I came home late one night and was accused of sleeping with my moms' man and I knew I couldn't stay. I found a place to go, packed up my things, and left. I was 19. Moving out changed my life forever. I was catching the bus at the time and the place I lived in was not too far from where my first rape took place. It was my understanding that the guy was in jail. One day coming home from work on the bus, the rapist gets on the bus walking straight towards me. At that moment, if I could have jumped off the bus while it was moving, I wouldn't be here today. That was a moment in time.

My life changed again. Is this really how life works, I thought. I remember telling myself, *"From here on out, I have to find a new way of living and letting go or I won't make it."* When I left home, I told myself, *"I wouldn't go back, as long as I'm living, I will not be on welfare and I will do what I can to help my family. I refuse to live the life I grew up in."* Well, I did have to go back home, but going back home is where I encountered my brothers and sisters in Christ from Crusader Baptist Church of God and joined the church. I did not end up on welfare and I did what I could to help my family. Helping my family at that time, unfortunately, caused me to go into debt. I did not know how to balance my finances or use credit cards in a manner that was helpful. I struggled to pay the essentials like rent, electricity, and phone… and I ended up filing for bankruptcy. As I learned to pray, I continued working, thanking God for my job, and trying to build a foundation for myself in the church. I continued to tell myself that welfare is not where it's at. What can I do, what should I do? I had to move a couple of times. Once because my roommate had stolen from me and wouldn't pay her portion of the rent. I felt lost and scared because my credit wasn't good. I found another roommate and for a little while it worked. But I backslid, yet I continued going to church. I was trying to get things together mentally, physically, and emotionally and one day I encountered the same rapist again. This time, I confronted him, forgave him, and that day I was set free. To God Be

All the Glory! I still had a ways to go. I was battling depression, oppression, sexual demons, and fear.

What's next Jesus? Is my life over? Is it just beginning? Where do I belong? I don't think I can take anymore! I began screaming, yelling, and crying. Thank God for the Church. I continued going to work. My job had us taking training on planning out our goals and visions. So, I did a vision board and had to put items on a board, showing what I wanted to accomplish. Go to college and get my degree, get a promotion, buy a home, get married, have children, buy a car, go on a cruise, and write a book. I have accomplished all but three of those visions! A shift happened in my life at that moment. Those goals became real targets for me to achieve. I started acting on my goals, listed on my vision board. The first priority goal was to enroll in college to enhance my career. I started going to Montgomery College. It felt good to know that I could attend college. My mom had gotten sick, she had heart issues, and went into a diabetic semi-coma. I began praying and when she came out, I was the only one she could remember, so I had to help her reestablish her relationship with all her children.

"*What's next?*", I asked. I had to fight to keep my job because they were trying to fire me. However, my supervisor decided that she would help me keep my job, and I even ended up getting my promotion! I continued building my relationship with God in a way that I trusted Him for everything in my life. I became celibate so that

I could prepare for my husband and children. It was my faith. Everyone was getting married or having babies and I figured I was ready. So, I began to prepare. It was a faith walk.

My life once again drastically changed. I was blessed with a new home, a car, with a promotion and I, continued in school, but the Lord had other plans. I attended seminary schools and received my associate, bachelor's, master's, and doctoral degrees and even became a pastor in the process. But what about my husband? What about children? I was getting older. *"God you said in your word, if I ask, I will receive."* Well, the man I thought would be my husband decided he didn't want to be. Broke my heart, and after that everyone around me was getting engaged or married and I was asked to officiate. Then it happened. I was having so many issues with my womb. Fibroids had to be removed. After that surgery, the unthinkable happened. I had emergency surgery which consisted of a full hysterectomy which meant that I would not be able to have any children. Of course, I prayed, believing God, that it would not happen. But not only did I have to have surgery, but the doctor that took care of me while I was in the hospital was pregnant! And she was the one who came to tell me that I would not be able to have children. I did not know what was going to happen, but I knew that I did not want my faith to waiver and that I wouldn't walk away from God. I went straight into menopause and depression for at least three years, but I never stopped preaching, teaching, or praying. I felt like I lost a big part of myself, but God loved me enough to bring me children that love me and care for me. I still have my moments when I wish I could have carried, but the more I leaned and depended on Jesus the easier it became to let my heart love children that I did not birth. If you ever find yourself in this place, build on your faith and it will carry you to your next destination. I still have my job, my ministry, and my life. I am blessed!

Love Notes:

Love Notes:

Author Gerly Sapphire Harris

Author Gerly Sapphire Harris

Gerly Sapphire Harris was born and raised in Brooklyn, New York and currently resides in the nation's capital. Mrs. Harris is married and has one awesome son, one stepdaughter, and one grandson. Mrs. Harris has always been the recipient of her family's love which started with her parents Odette Marc (*Rest in Power Mommy*), her father Veraty Marc, and her siblings Nicole Salomon, Frantz Labiessier, Beatrice Guilbaud, Valerie Adeluwoye, Jovanna Yafah Marc, and Andre Marc. *Love* has played a vital role in the life of Mrs. Harris and she thanks her extended family for being a vital part of her life, legacy, and journey of Mrs. Harris. The beloved extended family are as follows: Betty Harris 'Momma Harris' (Men & Women On the Move for Christ, Inc), Rosie Judy Jeanty, Willie Ramirez, Corey King, Sabrina Davis, Howard 'Howie' Harris, Carla Bryan, Capree Junior 'Onederful' Green, Tara Johnson, Derrick 'Powerful' Green, Nicole 'Brown-Eyes' Brunner, Tuwana Gomez, Trevor 'Everlasting' Hinds, Camille Jackson, Carlos Brown, Tina, Prince, Monica Bailey, Davon 'Fudge' Harris, Alberto 'Panama' Greene, two brothers Mike and Cliff, Marshall 'Un' King, Fat Patrick Sanon (RIP), and Rodney Frazier (RIP).

Mrs. Harris currently works at the United States Department of Health and Human Services, under the Health Resources and Services Administration (HRSA), although this job does not adequately describe all of who she is. Mrs. Harris is an advocate of woman's health and a proponent of the inclusion of all populations, especially individuals with disabilities. The disability culture is a growing and dynamic community that is often overlooked as it relates to the promotion of good health, education, and women's empowerment.

As a person with a physical disability, Mrs. Harris realizes that she can positively impact society by conducting workshops, participating in conferences, and joining various women's organizations to help break through barriers and demolish stereotypes. Mrs. Harris has come to understand that her success, as a woman with a disability, could help inspire people from all walks of life. Her desire to help others and make a difference in the world is far more than a whim; it's her passion.

Mrs. Harris has a Bachelor's Degree in Professional Studies and a Masters in Educational Psychology from Howard University. She is currently pursuing her Doctorate in Psychology. She is a lifetime member of Psi Chi International Honor Society in Psychology and has done extensive research on the disability culture and tutored youths with disabilities.

Mrs. Harris has also conducted presentations at a number of conferences and forums pertaining to the disability culture throughout the Washington DC Metropolitan area and in New York. She is the former Washington, DC Chapter President for the National Association of Professional Women organization. Mrs. Harris is the National Committee Chair for the NCBW Culture of People with Disabilities Committee. She currently sits on the Board and was the former President for the Kiwanis Club of Northwest Washington, DC, and currently the President for the Kiwanis Club of Far East, where the focus area of both clubs focuses on the empowerment of children with disabilities. Mrs. Harris is a member of Eta Phi Beta Sorority, Inc., the President of the HRSA Employee Resource Group Council on Employees with Disabilities, and a member of the Metropolitan Women's Democratic Club. She is also an active member of NARFE and Chapter's National Legislation Chair. Mrs. Harris is an active member of The Daughters, an Auxiliary of A.E.O.N.M.S., Order of the Eastern Star, and writes for the Grand Lodge of the District of Columbia, Inc. PHA Masonic Digest.

She has a burning passion for the country of Haiti and Haitian people worldwide. She has traveled to Haiti as a part of a political envoy and she works tirelessly with different organizations to help improve the quality of life for the great citizens of Haiti. She has also traveled to South African in a missionary capacity and to Europe for educational and missionary purposes.

Mrs. Harris received a number of awards for her hard work and dedication from Blacks In Government Parklawn Chapter, National Congress of Black Women, National Association of Professional Women, HRSA ERG, Men Aiming Higher, Inc., just to name a few. Mrs. Harris continues to be a positive Social Change Agent for the Culture of People with Disabilites.

Love, Disability, and Acceptance

HER PERSPECTIVE~ Sapphire Harris

Love; love is something that we all are born with ~
Some utilize it and let it grow into a form of agape' love, which is mainly an unconditional type of love, while others leave their love to dry up ~
Love comes in many shapes and sizes, you can let it show through your actions without any sort of effort because when dealing with love,
It comes naturally for some, while other people have to work hard at it ~
You can also express love through sweet words of excellence ~
Love can destroy or build a person ~
It can be a benefit to others,
thus it depends on how one possesses their love ~
For at times, your love can lead a person to believe in one thing,
but the pureness of your heart in actuality is thinking of another ~
How does one endear love after being hurt by someone you love?
Having to go through all the stages of love,
Can one love again with the same measure? ~
Surely to say for some, the pain which is caused by another is used as a stepping stone, which helps bring forth a higher level of love,
Leaving no room for hate or any afflictions ~
Love, how can someone not practice such a gift, such affection, and admiration from feelings that comes deep within ~
The gratifications of being loved and embraced without any payment or ever feeling that, this person owes you something in return ~
Love, oh sweet love, love can conquer all evil, *Love.*

Along my life's journey, there have been highs, lows, and everything you can imagine in between. My journey has not always been predictable or easy to navigate but I have had three constant companions that have never left my side. **Love, disability, and acceptance** are as much part of my journey as the ground upon which I have traveled. At certain points of my journey, I could not always see them or feel their presence, but they have always been a part of me. **Love, disability, and acceptance** infused me with strength and energy when mine was at its lowest and a platform by which I could make a difference in the lives of those who would one day follow. The journey has not been easy, but it is mine and this is where my story begins.

I was born with one leg shorter than the other, and other physical abnormalities, which included Spinal Bifida and scoliosis. I had a stuttering challenge and attended speech therapy for many years. I also wrote backward but this was not the result of a learning disability, it was birthed out of necessity. As the youngest child, I figured that writing in this manner would allow me to keep my thoughts private until I was ready to share them. My love for writing and sharing my thoughts, in this form, began when I was a little girl. I did not want my siblings, who at the time did not completely understand me, critiquing my thoughts that had not been fully developed.

Another part of my early life consisted of surgeries and pain. Growing up, I had several surgeries, although none of them had the desired outcome of correcting the abnormalities of my spine or the length of my leg. I was three days old when I had my first surgery, undertaken to correct the unusual way my leg had developed. I had many challenges to overcome, and as I grew older, and discovering 'self-love' was perhaps the most difficult of them all.

Spending a great deal of time in hospitals before I spoke my first words had a massive residual impact on my life. It was impossible to attend school in a traditional manner when much of my energy was consumed with medical treatments. The physical challenges faced as an infant and during my early years lead many of the medical professionals working with me, to believe that I would never walk. My last surgery, around the age of seven, was the most challenging because it was nearly fatal. During this surgery I actually flatlined. It felt as if a part of me, the essence of who I was, started transitioning to the next level of spiritual existence, while a part of me remained rooted in this dimension. As I got older and developed a greater understanding of God's word, I believe that it was His love and purpose for my life that brought me back to life.

Love is a gift from God, released upon the earth for all of His creations to participate in and enjoy. Love is more than just a word or an internal sensation felt during intense moments; it is a living, breathing part of life. Love gives us wings and has the power to heal hurting hearts, relieve anxiety, and not only inspire creativity, but inspire greatness as well. Love adds a texture to life that makes it more worth living. Although you cannot always tell by what is taking place on a local or global level, love has the power to unite and uplift communities beyond measure. Love is all-powerful, it is ever-present, and it transcends all time and space. Love is something that we are all born with and into.

In a world filled with amazing and wonderfully unique creations, you would think that individuals whose bodies perform common functions in uncommon ways would be embraced. This would be ideal, but it is far from a reality for the millions of individuals throughout the world living with some form of disability. Instead of being lauded for bringing a unique perspective to every situation, that a member within the culture of people with disabilities finds themselves in, either by invitation or in many cases by inviting themselves as necessary, the differences are often seen and used as a reason for scorn. While individuals within the disability community may walk differently, talk differently, and approach life in a manner different than the majority population, *(which is the able-bodied community for the sake of discussion)*, this is a culture that desires and deserves to experience love in all aspects of life.

As mentioned earlier, love is a gift from God. It saturates all the earth for everyone blessed to be alive and able to experience it. Love is everywhere at all times, and the magnitude of its reach cannot be overstated. However, even though love is all-encompassing, many of the love tanks of individuals, we cross paths with each day, are hovering on empty. With all of the love in the world available to each of us, some go without. We, as a society, are living in a sea of love and loving possibilities, but many are not experiencing the love that is available to the extent possible. While the issue of embracing and experiencing love appears to be a problem in the able-bodied community, it is reaching catastrophic levels in the disabled community. Part of the challenge we face in the able-bodied and disabled communities alike may be rooted in society's misunderstanding and lack of appreciation for the sacred gift of true love.

We live in a society where most people may not fully love and appreciate themselves for their beauty or how they were created. That lack of self-love is even greater in some instances within the disability community. The culture of people with disabilities is often misunderstood, and at times people have a tendency to fill in the blanks, in their mind, with information that is totally off base. As a result, when a person within the disability community does something noteworthy, people act as if they have seen an extraterrestrial being. The culture of people with disabilities, *my culture*, is exceedingly strong, filled with potential, that will continue to manifest for all the world to see. Part of my life's purpose is to help integrate the culture of people with disabilities into the mainstream and help the world see the great possibility that this culture has. I work extremely hard, on a daily basis, to bring a greater level of awareness as it relates to the capability, capacity, and potential of this dynamic culture.

As much as we were created to receive and share love with others, I believe we must first learn to love and accept ourselves for who we are and the special way that we were created. If there was a second stanza to the Greek aphorism, *"know thy self"*, it would also read, *"love thy self."* The love of self that is spoken of here is not conceded or boastful in any way. It is the type of love that is referenced in 1 Corinthians 13:4-8, which reads, *"Love suffers long and is kind; love does not envy; love does not parade itself, is not puffed up; does not behave rudely, does not seek its own, is not provoked, thinks no evil; does not rejoice in iniquity, but rejoices in the truth; bears all things, believes all things, hopes all things, endures all things. Love never fails."* This passage of Scripture speaks to the power of love that we all possess.

If love is the key, how does one learn to love themselves if they were born with or have become disabled at some point in life? Does love look or feel different within the culture of people with disabilities? Most of our first lessons on love, how best to express and receive love, are learned through the love we receive from our family members, our caregivers, and what we see or hear in our day-to-day lives. We also learned from observing the actions and inactions of those around us. This is an area of challenge for the disability community because some differences are not easily embraced. History has taught us that it is often difficult to accept and love what you don't understand. This viewpoint is unfortunate and could prevent exposure to individuals and ideas that could provide new insights, help shift thoughts, and introduce a life-changing love.

My life, the impact that I have had thus far, and my achievements can be traced back to the family that I was born into by God's Grace. Being born into a Caribbean family who saw opportunity when others saw obstacles was a blessing that words cannot describe. My family demanded and expected the best from me, and they would not allow me to feel sorry for myself or use the disability that I was born with as an excuse. They did not necessarily understand how I felt as a person with a disability, but they saw something in me that the disability could not conceal or erase. My family and close friends loved me beyond measure, and that is why I am, the person I am today. They may not have understood the pain that I and other members of the culture of people with disabilities experienced on a daily basis, but they loved and accepted me just the way I was created. My family and friends never showed me sympathy for the challenges I, as a person born with a disability encountered. Empathy and compassion yes, sympathy – never.

Love was the foundation upon which my life was built. Love might not remove the challenging issues of life that we face, but it plays a vital role in overcoming them. Everyone was born with a burden to carry, and in many instances that challenge is one of the keys to our destiny. Reframing how we look at these challenges goes a long way towards discovering the solution. My family never made the issue being faced bigger than they were. During the challenging stretches in my life, their love sustained me until I was strong enough to keep moving, no matter what was taking place within my environment. They reminded me of their love and encouraged me to seek the answers.

My parents taught me to create my own life narrative and to live into it daily. They taught me to believe that a world of possibilities and love was always available if you believed. My family taught me that others might not have the best intentions for me and may try to lock me into a category filled with limitations because of their perception of me as a person with a disability, but the sky is the limit as long as I continued to believe, love, and accept myself as a child of the Most-High God, the Creator of this world. At this time, I had to be very mindful of the words that I accepted from others, as well as words I spoke to myself. Because if I received negative words, it could be a bit difficult to release them. At that point in my life, I had the voice of dysfunction and the voice of my destiny battling for dominance in the space between my ears. The voice that won would be the one that I let dominate this precious territory. In battles such as this, I found love to be the most valuable soldier at my disposal.

Managing that inner voice is vital to sustained success for both the able-bodied and the disabled alike. Allowing the voice of dysfunction, the freedom to disrupt our internal conversations, will only lead to more dysfunction. If the voice of dysfunction is the loudest, it will impact what we hear. The things that we listen to, internally and externally, we have a tendency to believe. What we believe, we will act upon. When this happens we are usually recreating out of our dysfunctional past which will probably only to more dysfunction. If we choose to listen to and honor the voices of our destiny, it will lead to a totally different path. This path leads to success, love, and acceptance.

Grooming others from the able-bodied and disabled community has become my focus. This is important to me because the lessons I have learned can reduce the time others have between their dreams and reality. My desire is to teach others about the power of love, disability, and acceptance in a way that will increase understanding and unity. I want all the world to know that love equates to possibility and it is available to each one of us. This love does not tire, does not get bored, and never fails. It is also important to groom others because as Bishop T.D. Jakes and others have said, *there is no true enduring success without a successor.* Our difficult lessons can be the stepping stone used by others to ascend the latter of success.

Creating a platform to help train the next generation of global leaders within the disability community, is part of the natural progression of this culture. Love, disability, and acceptance inspired me to fully embrace myself and motivated me to live a life worthy of emulation.

Love…

Love Notes:

Author La'Kenya S. Walter

Author La'Kenya S. Walter

Author La'Kenya S. Walter is an accomplished Financial Specialist with over 15 years in the financial industry, serving both the private and public sectors. Her financial background includes banking and financial analysis for loans and grants.

Ms. Walter works well with senior corporate executives and provides consultation and financial guidance. She has insight and proven results in grant writing. Based on her knowledge and skills, she can help an organization thrive and reach its financial potential. In July 2019, Ms. Walter started her own consulting business, The Oracle Consulting Group, LLC. The mission of the organization is to provide support in business organization and coaching.

Ms. Walter is an alumna of Old Dominion University and Liberty University. She holds a Bachelor of Science in Business Administration, as well as a Master of Business Administration. She recently earned a Certificate in Women's Entrepreneurship from Cornell University.

Ms. Walter serves her community with a servant's heart. She sits on numerous boards, both as an officer and advisor. Her involvement includes: Commissioner on the Charles County Commission for Women, Past State President of Business and Professional Women of Maryland, Treasurer and Finance Chair of the Board of Directors for Community Advocate for Families and Youth, member of Washington Carver Chapter of Blacks in Government, Charter member of Charles County Section of The National Council of Negro Women, Inc., Chair of the Advisory Council for American Minority Veterans Research Project, and a member of Delta Sigma Theta Sorority, Inc. Ms. Walter is a native of the Eastern Shore of Virginia and has a fur baby Braxton.

Dedication from Author La'Kenya Walter:

I dedicate this chapter, my first step to *"unmasking"*, to my foundation: my family. I love and adore my sisters: Chalarra, Temeko, and Alexandra. They are my backbone and biggest cheerleaders.
To my three heartbeats, my nieces Ja'Miah, Tekierra, and Kenadee, I hope that along with your parents we are leaving a legacy that you can all be proud to be a part of.

To my mommy Linda, *thank you*. Words cannot explain my gratitude and thankfulness to you. You are my calming spirit.
Daddy: thank you for always showing me that I am a true daddy's girl.

Ganny and Uncle Tony, my heart hurts tremendously with your absence but you instilled in me my love for people, the community and drive to want better.

Contact Ms. Walter at:
Email: lakenyasw@gmail.com
Instagram: @Kenyasw

Unmasking Single Love

When I hear the word *"Love"* it takes on so many different meanings to me. God is love, family is love, relationships symbolize love, and for some material things define love. But what hits close and personal to me is the love I have for others and receiving that same love in return. By the time you read my story, I will have just turned the, oh so fabulous 40! Turning this milestone birthday has sparked some deep thoughts about where I am in life. One area, in particular, is my singleness and the preparation for changing this season.

I am one of four girls. All my sisters are MARRIED. My best friend of almost fifteen years- MARRIED. Me-SINGLE! That's right, single, forty, no kids and have never been married. Yes, I am single until my last name is changed. *Humph!* Anyway, as forty drew closer, I found myself irritated, frustrated, and thinking, *"why the heck haven't I gotten married yet and found that love that God describes in the Bible?"* My conclusion is that it isn't my time yet. I always tell my inner circle that I know how God works on my behalf, so when *he* finds me it is going to blow my mind!

I love *love*! I love that black love, that Agape love. Now don't get it twisted, I have dated and dated and dated. Some I thought would be *"the one"* and some of those jokers, I later learned, were STEPPING-STONES. I have fallen in love many times and have had men fall "in love" but couldn't commit to the next step. My life reminds me of lyrics from one of my favorite artists, H.E.R. *"Learn me or I was a LESSON"*. Despite all of this, I still push forward because my belief is that this is my preparation for my life partner. I am determined to do it right, whole, and together.

I love hard, give my all, I am loyal, and that *ride or die*. But for some reason, the relationships all end the same way; me being frustrated and walking away without an explanation or complete closure. Sadly, I never remain friends once the connection is lost. Yet I push forward. Since I desire the love that I give, I stepped back and decided that I needed to focus on myself. I had a man ask me, *"What do you bring to the table?"* Those that know me know that the last thing I do is talk about myself or brag about my accomplishments because there is so much more to me than just that. But since he asked, I can easily roll off my credentials. I am a Financial/Career-Branch Chief at a federal government agency, I own my own home, vehicles, retirement plan-CHECK. Spiritually- I know *who* I serve and my God has me grounded! I am that Proverbs 31 woman-CHECK. Emotionally- I am still working on that, but I am an encourager, loyal and supportive-CHECK. Physically- I am getting back in the gym to be healthier-CHECK. Oh, and I have a Bachelor of Science in

Business Administration, Masters of Business Administration, and a Certificate in Women's Entrepreneurship from Cornell University- CHECK. On the flip side, I am aware that I struggle with insecurities: trust, an empath, and time (I am heavily involved in the community). I feel that I bring a whole heck of a lot to the table (side-eye and clutch pearls). Sir, I AM the TABLE and bring a hearty appetite! Nonetheless, I understood his statement and it was very valid to ask. As I just made that statement, I wonder if some of my struggles, in finding love, could be because of intimidation. I require a confident Alpha male that can handle this Boss Diva. On a positive note, the areas that I display a weakness have been identified and the work has begun, more on that later.

Don't get me wrong, I am an independent, strong, and smart woman. I am all about women's empowerment because we do rule the world. We can do anything we set our mind to, but sometimes, even the "*shero*" needs a hero! Being married doesn't define who I am, but I do wish to share life and all it has to offer with a soulmate. I desire to experience the type of love that only God can create between two people.

Now that we have gotten who I am and my point of view about being single, grab your coffee, tea, cocktail, or mocktail and let me tell you a little about my single journey (embracing/owning it).

Lesson #1: Puppy Love

I grew up in a small town. Everybody knows everyone. I was a college student who still found a reason to return home every weekend. Well, one of the local *"street"* boys was on a mission. His mission *"Operation Kiki"*. I dismissed his advances for a long time because my Ganny instilled in us to always stay focused on our education. At that point in my life, I was scared of everything. After months and months of seeking me out, I finally decided to entertain him. We never made anything official, (red flag) and I knew there were other women, but I enjoyed the attention and went along with it. I fell in love, him not so much. I allowed for this *"sneaky link"* to go on for years!!! I was young, immature, and only saw things one way. It took a health scare for me to decide that this was not the love or lifestyle that I wanted to live, so I had to get out. By this time, I had graduated college so when my oldest sister and brother-in-law offered for me to come and live with them to find a job I strongly considered. This was now my time to make that change. Being me and my way of escape, I packed up and walked away without a word; reflecting, thank you Jesus for delivering me. STEPPING-STONE #1. LESSON: Maturity

Lesson #2 Shared Love.

Fast forward, my best friend and I decided we were going to live our best lives and embark on my first international trip. Cancun was the destination. Somehow we ended up on a cruise to Bermuda. I would have never picked this location but again, God was in the midst, walking me through my "stepping-stones". I met a very tall, handsome man from the Caribbean and wooo, I fell hard. I have always had a thing for older men, that's another story for another time, but he was laying it on thick. He had me all in. One stipulation, he lived in another country and worked on the ship. There were so many red flags right there. I sailed on this *"ship love"* for about 3 years, only seeing each other a couple of times a year. I only dated him...silly me, but hey I was *"in love"*. I would pray, *"if this is not it, Lord show me in black in white."* Not long after that prayer, I was in his email because the dummy had asked me to help him check it before (don't men know we are super sleuths/archeologists) and I came across an email from a woman. I reached out to this lady and we had a nice, long, and very informative conversation. He basically was loving several women in the U.S. Honestly, this one hit me hard because I was blinded by what I thought was *love* so I did not see the red flags. I was sad for weeks. My best friend said, *"get your s*** together and move forward...you are better than this."* So I took her advice, charged it to the game, and shut dating down. STEPPING-STONE #2 LESSON: You are enough.

Lesson #3- Starting Over Love

Fast forward to 2012. I was now living in Charlottesville, VA. We had just lost our Ganny and my baby sister was graduating from college. When I watched her walk across the stage, I then realized it was time for me to go back to school and get my masters. I did just that. In November 2013 my best friend told me to pick a weekend getaway to celebrate my upcoming birthday. For some odd reason, I chose Washington, DC. Back then I didn't know a thing about DC. I was still in my grad program and that had been my focus for the last year, so where I went the computer went. Anyhow, she made me put the computer away, that crisp Saturday morning, and we headed to lunch in Chinatown. As we were finishing lunch, randomly I said to her *"I am ready to start dating again"*. She was shocked and started firing off questions. We discussed it and that was that, or so I thought. We left the restaurant and went to a museum.

During our tour, a gentleman approached me making small talk. We exchanged info and I left. I told my best friend, *"Dang, God heard that and went to work lol."* He and I dated, long-distance (again nothing official) for about a year. I was back and forth to DC often. He may have come to Charlottesville once. Red flag. I graduated from graduate school in 2014 and an opportunity for me to move to the Maryland/DC area popped up. I was all over it. Now, I was closer to him and I thought this was it. I soon found out that we clearly were not equally yoked. Knowing this, I still hung in there, not even living up to the standards and boundaries I had set. God kept showing me differently, but I was doing what I wanted and not what God wanted. I repeated and stayed in this one-sided relationship. I prayed for something to change. And it did. Lesson #4 came along and in true La'Kenya fashion, starting over, Love #3 was dropped without a phone call, email, or text. STEPPING-STONE #3. LESSON: Perseverance

Lesson/Blessing#4-Soul Tie Love.

I am a believer that God does all things for a reason, but baby, a soul tie love is powerful! At the time of our paths crossing, I was new to *"The Divine Nine"* (comprised of the 9 Black Greek Letter organizations that make up the National Pan-Hellenic Council) and was invited to a celebration. When I saw him, I was instantly drawn in. He spoke so eloquently, a complete gentleman, dressed sharp, and smelled oh so good. I never initiate or offer a dude my phone number, but I was not letting this man slip by. Something pulled me to him, at that chance of a meeting. I think I even shocked myself when I told him here is my number and we can see the area together sometimes. A couple of months went by before we finally connected to hang out. He was checking all the boxes: educated, driven, career, God-fearing, gentle, wanted to know me, and most importantly, made me feel safe. He knew, encouraged, and understood my career goals, my desire for a life partner, and the hunger I had to do more. It was going well and as much as I was telling myself not to fall and to take it slow, I did just the opposite. Dang it! I had fallen back in love. This was not part of the plan. My family (because he was now entangled in family events) adores him. Just one thing, why hadn't we moved closer to changing things. The answer I came up with was that we both needed work. In this instance, he was struggling with his own inner issues, one being commitment. When you are wrestling with yourself, not even a soul tie can compete with it. For me, the battle was trust. It was there, in the beginning, but along the way, the actions and lack thereof led to me having doubts.

Our connection was so strong that we could have those deep conversations without any misunderstanding. I believed we played/thrived off each other strengths. The energy was electrifying, but again, something was still missing. I think that in some sense I scared him. I pushed him to want more, do more, be more. We have traveled, celebrated promotions, grieved, faced health situations, and had disagreements. There came a time in our "relationship" that we were tested. That became a rough time period for me. Loyalty, strength, and that soul tie kept me still. I also realized a previous flag had raised its head yet again…certain aspects of his life were being kept from me. As we worked through that test, it became evident that the soul tie we had was something that I knew I had to investigate. Realizing this connection, I paused and knew it was time to have a come-to-Jesus meeting with myself. When I met him, I had refused to repeat Lessons 1, 2, and 3. I reflected on all the past relationships and wanted to do this right, this time because I felt that he was different.

His love for me is something that I may not fully understand or even uncover, but I know there is love and respect there. Our love language is mystifying. He became my inspiration and triggered me to set sight on what is most important in my life right now and do the work to be a better version of myself. I must be whole in order to be whole for my spouse. The lesson I took away from him is that I shouldn't take things for face value. I am now confident when it is time, there will be no question in what I bring to the table. It will reflect in my character, my strength, and my presence. The blessing is that I am forever grateful to him for building me up and helping this *Doll* to develop into a *Diva*. For helping me to identify my love rubric, it starts with me loving myself and do the work inside of myself. I have embraced my singleness, blossomed, and now am ready to see how this Lesson/Blessing turns out…his blessing or his lesson.

I want to leave these closing words of encouragement to all my single ladies: stay content in knowing who you are. Love will come. I am a believer. Dating isn't easy. Being single can be rewarding, but also some challenges. We all desire and deserve to be loved. But not just any love. I want that love to be pure, genuine, and blessed by God. Until that day, let's love on ourselves a little more: take the single trip, go to dinner alone, date 3-5 guys (safely), and build our empire. This hopeless romantic waits patiently. I am embarking on my next chapter from Miss to Mrs. Yes, I am speaking it into existence. I will continue to embrace my singleness, live out loud in my season, and do the work to be a better me. God, I am thankful for the stepping-stones and lessons that have led me to **Unmasking Single Love.** Stay tuned......

Love Notes:

Author La'Kisha Lacey

Author La'Kisha Lacey

La'Kisha L. Lacey is a native Washingtonian and is currently residing in the District of Columbia. She really enjoys traveling, shopping, and spending time with her family. La'Kisha is married to her lifelong "LOVE" and together they have one son and one granddaughter.

She is a 20-year veteran and ranking officer of a local Fire and EMS Department and is traveling on a journey of self-improvement and dynamic growth. With the desire to serve and help, she manages the Community Outreach Division of the fire service and serves on several citywide appointed boards. She also has the distinct honor of being a part of various community-based organizations that pride themselves on their charitable works within the community.

Better known to many of her colleagues and friends, Kisha's greatest accomplishments are her marriage and enduring the struggles that have gotten her to 31 years within the relationship, and being not only a mother, but a great mother. She also prides herself on being able to openly speak her truth and acknowledge that no one is always right. While traveling that path, she has learned that while one is enjoying the other is suffering.

What does the future hold for Kisha? Well, she plans to go back to school and finish her bachelor's degree. Switching her focus of studies from Mortuary Science to Fine Arts, and Photography, to be exact. She says that she has a career that she loves, and wouldn't trade it for anything. However, she has a desire to embark upon a second career that is a bit more peaceful but fulfilling to her.

You ask the question, "*Why did Kisha write this chapter?*" Well, everyone has flaws and no one is perfect. It is very hard to struggle through your own issues and to also save face in public. I am perfectly flawed and know in my heart that some need to hear that every storm does end in destruction."

Email: kishawaters27@gmail.com
Facebook – @Kishas Astarr
Instagram - @the1theonlymrsh2os

Because He Unconditionally Loves *ME*

Young Love

For many, LOVE is a word associated with an emotion that is often misunderstood. As for me, love started out as something that I wanted to experience and share, but I really didn't know how. I was blessed to find someone who saw past my drama and loved me unconditionally. It was a love that lived deep within him that kept us united when my actions were pushing us apart. There were many days when I felt like I had lost him, and even worse than that was when I felt like I had lost a part of myself as well. Fortunately, there was a love inside of him that was bigger than everything that we encountered.

Our love story began a long time ago, 1990 to be exact. The phone conversations we had were always on 100, and the chemistry was amazing. Imagine two kids coming of age, lacking in knowledge, but trying to talk grown folk shit! When that magical day came, the day that a 13-year-old girl and a 14-year-old boy finally met in person for the first time, he uttered those game-changing words, *"You're gonna be my girl"*. At that moment, my world changed.

I was smitten *"with love"* at the age of 13. This occurred in April 1990 and it would be more than a year before I saw him again. We were apart so long because he lived in Maryland and I lived in Washington D.C., but we communicated by phone every day for hours at a time. It was distant love, 1990's style at its best. This story may seem like the classic tale of girl meets boy, they fall in love, and live happily ever after, but not exactly. There is some truth in that narrative because as of April 2021, we've been together for 31 years, but there is more to the story. When we first met, I had no idea it would become a lifetime assignment. However, it has been the most rewarding endeavor I have ever embarked upon, because of the life lessons learned.

Our roller coaster ride began to plunge as the calendar moved forward towards the year 1991. I was in high school, and we were still in a distant relationship, but we were even closer than before. My boyfriend and his cousin surprised me by attending a basketball game at my school. I was in the bleachers with a male schoolmate who liked me more than I realized. The moment I saw my boyfriend; I went to sit with him. This moment signaled the beginning of the drama-filled portion of our relationship. He was angered by this scenario, yet *"He Unconditionally Loved Me."* What came next was not my plan, but I got pregnant my senior year and delivered a beautiful baby boy one month before graduation and still walked across the stage as one of the top 10 students. Not top 10%, but one of the top 10 students in my graduating class! I was on the move, and nothing could stop me. As the real work of raising a baby began, I thank God for my VILLAGE. I am so grateful for the support that I received from my VILLAGE as I was a young mother, who could barely care for herself at the time. While raising a child as a teenager is a difficult undertaking, I had someone who cared for us both emotionally and financially. We didn't have public assistance, a housing voucher, or food stamps. Nope, we lived with my family, and my boyfriend worked to provide for his new family.

Years later, I was living in my own apartment, and I had male company visiting me one evening. My boyfriend walked in and saw me sitting on the bed in my pajamas talking to my male guest. Although strictly platonic, it was not a good look for a person that was in a committed relationship. I was so scared that he was going to hurt me, but that is not in his nature. I can honestly say that *"He Unconditionally Loved Me."*

After being together for years, eleven years into romance to be exact, I found myself in a bad situation once again. We were lying in the bed and people were outside, and someone yelled up to my window. I wasn't expecting anyone, but given my track record, this was the straw that broke the camel's back. After a very heated discussion, my boyfriend walked out on me and my son, and I felt broken. Bobby Womack said it best, *"If you think you're lonely now, wait until tonight, girl"*. As bad as I felt, I couldn't show it because that's not who I was. My image was that of a strong, fierce, goal-driven person, and I could not let that go.

I was strong in public, but behind the scenes, there were tears and begging for forgiveness. Nothing I did changed his decision. I hoped having sex would fix all our problems, and he would come home. Boy, I could not have been more wrong. My mindset towards reconciling didn't change until I saw something that I could not unsee. I was using the bathroom at his house and saw evidence of another woman's presence. My love instantly turned to hate, and I felt physically, emotionally, and mentally broken. I wanted nothing more to do with him, not even if it was pertaining to our son. Every day, I woke up feeling miserable and wished that I hadn't awakened at all. This went on for months, but I PUT MY BIG GIRL PANTIES ON AND DEALT WITH IT. No one knew the shame and pain that filled my heart.

After accepting that he was moving on with his life without me, I soon began to "live" again; how I did it only God knows. Explaining to our son why Mommy and Daddy weren't together anymore, wasn't an option. I couldn't tell our son that his mother's choices lead to his father's mistrust, and he had finally had enough of my shit and walked out on *"ME"*. So, like any other strong-willed woman in my position, I had to survive because failure was not an option. Surviving meant cleaning up my mess and becoming the best version of myself. I focused on my new career, working a second job, and being a successful single mom. My desire to become my best self had nothing to do with the father of my child. He was a great dad and took phenomenal care of our son, but my anger prevented me from accepting anything from him. My pride would not let me ask him for anything, so I worked two full-time jobs instead.

I grew personally and purchased a home and a new car ON MY OWN. I finished school, and emotionally I moved on with my life and began to date. I discovered *"me"* and I liked it. Keep in mind that I had been with my *"boyfriend"* since I was 13 years old, and I didn't really know life without him. My son was born when I was seventeen, so I had never been grown and single. My son's well-being was also my number one priority, even with my busy schedule and relationship drama. By God's grace, my son always saw me as a loving mother. I wasn't having promiscuous or unsafe sex, but I was enjoying my life as a single woman.

One of my happiest single parent moments came when my son told me that he didn't like his father's girlfriend and didn't want to go back to his dad's house anymore. My response was probably the same as anyone who hadn't properly processed their emotional pain, I said, "OKAY". Was this the anger of a still bitter woman or simply a mother's love? I honestly don't know. I just know that at the time it felt good.

Now, for the unexpected and no longer desired reunion. It seems like yesterday. I arrived home one evening to find my son's father *(Yes, I was that parent who needed to know that for any reason my son could come home)* was in my house, lying on my floor covered in blood. His cousin had been killed two days after my grandmother died and all I could do was console him because I could feel every stitch of the pains that riddled his body. This is where our lives took a turn for the unknown. I did not welcome him into my home, and certainly not back into my life, but here he was. I didn't know whether to be happy that what I had prayed so long for was finally happening or be mad that after years of struggling to get over him, I was right back at square one.

The Do-Over

The evolution of our relationship went from young love to pregnancy and childbirth; then there was deceit, separation, desperation, hurt, and heartbreak, and then we were back together again. Was I ready to alter my lifestyle after I had to learn to be independent and self-sufficient? How do I adjust my life and my love for the man who had done nothing but "*LOVE*" me? I struggled to go back to school, build a career, purchase my own home, and create a positive environment for my child. Was I ready to forgive the one that I truly loved and scarred, even though he left me? Could I allow him back into my life and have what my heart wanted, but didn't feel that I deserved, or should I remain in the same status? The second option would put me in the "baby's momma category", which I did not want? Boundaries were never verbalized, nor were expectations made known, but from that day until this, when I wake up each morning, he is lying beside me.

Happiness filled my heart until the day I returned from a cruise and found emails on my computer of conversations between him and some woman, and then later, text messages from another woman. She said that she missed him, among other things, and I was not sure how to process what I read. Was this payback for the years of foolishness that I'd put him through or a sign? I was not sure at that time how to proceed, but it gave me an excuse to continue to be unfaithful.

There was, and remains a sense of suspicion that has been earned. I believe it is because of insecurity. I was caught in a less than righteous position more than once, and still, I tried to lie and deny it. I need my husband more than either one of us realized. I am a woman with certain requirements, and attention from him tops the list. I NEED flowers and gifts just to affirm I'm on his mind. I want, need, and deserve to be SPOILED. Perhaps I got involved in awkward situations because I wasn't receiving those things in one way or another. It seems like outside activities such as coaching, and hanging with his friends took precedence over me, but that was just my biased perception.

Still Working

You know, there's a saying *"If you want to make God laugh, tell him your plan."* Well, I must've made God's belly ache with laughter, time and time again. I tried doing things my way and every time I did, HE stopped me dead in my tracks. The last time God reminded me how blessed I've been over the past 31 years, occurred on May 25, 2020, at 5:00 am. Pain riddled my body from head to toe. My chest felt like an elephant sat on me, fluids were leaving my body in every way imaginable. This all happened during the height of the pandemic, and I didn't know if I was having a heart attack or dying from COVID-19. At my most vulnerable moment, he was there for me. I had to depend on the man who for so many years had been in my corner, to wipe my behind, wash me up, clothe me and rush me to the emergency room; only to be told that I had to have emergency surgery. Let me pause for just a minute, while everyone is trying to figure out what any of this has to do with "*LOVE*". Well, let me tell you, "*LOVE*" slept on the phone with me every night for seven consecutive days because he wanted me to feel his presence even though he was not allowed to be with me at the hospital. "*LOVE*" cried when he didn't know if I was going to live or die. "*LOVE*" couldn't visit, so he sat in the parking lot of the hospital staring at the building while he spoke to me on the phone. God used this life-or-death situation to open my eyes fully, and I finally got it. This man has loved me unconditionally through all my mess, which God has turned into my message. The love that I have, and always wanted, has been here for 31 years!

My man has not always been innocent, and things happen, but I refuse to play the victim. The interesting entanglement of love that we've shared over the years has been like God's classroom because He has used my husband to help me see how much I craved attention. God also showed me how much I desired the number one spot when that spot should be reserved for God. I am still a work in progress. I now know my triggers, and I am working hard to neutralize them. I often wonder about my husband's actions and possible infidelities, but I can't worry about things that I can't control. If this marriage is going to work, I must focus on being the best wife that "I" can be. While it may look good on the outside, no one sees the challenges that we encounter behind closed doors. Suspicion is ever-present and everything that occurs is magnified and scrutinized. There is nothing normal about our relationship and that is okay.

In a toxic relationship, there is often the role of the victim and the role of the aggressor. The role of the aggressor is not usually cast in a favorable light, so people often claim the victim for fear of being judged. Well, I admit that through all the ups and downs, I have been the major source of our problems. I can only account for what I contributed, good or bad to our relationship. Even with all that has taken place in our relationship from lies to infidelity, my

"*HUSBAND*" has never given up on me. I will never tell anyone that growing up in a relationship and struggling through a marriage has been easy.

What I will tell you is, **"But GOD!"**

Love Notes:

Author Lashena Shields

Author Lashena Shields

Lashena Shields was born in Baltimore, Maryland, and has been residing in Delaware for the last three years. She has one daughter to who she devotes all her time to. They both like traveling, cooking, and dancing. Lashena obtained her Bachelor's degree in Criminal Justice Administration and Management from the University of Phoenix. Lashena has over 21 years in Law Enforcement and loves what she does day-to-day.

Lashena's path in life had its ups and downs but she never gave up. Lashena wants people who, like Lashena, are going through similar situations to understand that it's okay to take a chance and learn from your mistakes. People looking in from the outside would think that Lashena's life was perfect, but if you ask her, she would tell you that she's human and will make mistakes, but she will learn from them. Lashena's motto is: *Live, Love, and Enjoy life to the fullest.*

Facebook- @Lashena.Shields
Instagram- @LashendaShields

NOT THE RIGHT HUSBAND FOR ME

God Shined a Light On Me

Never *judge a book by its cover.* If I didn't tell you my story you wouldn't even know what I have been through in my short 42 years on this Earth. I married my first husband at 21, and he was 33. I thought he was the man for me, but in life, you have to find out the hard way. He had a couple of kids, and later down the line, I found out he struggled with a drug and alcohol addiction. In life, you can't fix people or save them if they don't want help. I became pregnant by him and was told I should think about abortion because he didn't want any more kids. I thought to myself, *"If my own husband can tell me to have an abortion, he truly doesn't love me."* So I made the decision to way have an abortion, and the day I went forth with it, he was nowhere to be found. I went by myself and made a life-changing decision that still to this day I don't regret what I decided to do with my body. Later that night I began to bleed more than usual, so I called a friend to take me back to the hospital. Come to find out, the abortion clinic didn't get everything. I never forgave my husband for his lack of support during this trying time. As a result, the love that had been was gone. I tried to get him the help he needed but his addictions were more important to him than our marriage. When he didn't seek the help I tried to provide for him, I decided to file for divorce, change my locks and move on with my life. On my wedding day, God had spoken to me as I walked down the aisle. *"This isn't the man for you"*, and I didn't listen. In life, some people have to learn the hard way, just as I did.

Moving on, I met my second husband, years later on an island in the middle of the Pacific Ocean. I moved there for my job to build my career. I was only there for a month when I met the man that would become my husband. We were just like the saying - *"opposites attract."* I think at that point in my life, I *allowed* him to ask me out on a date. Looking back on everything, I realize that I was depressed that I was so far from home with no family, only coworkers, and some new friends I had met. I should have picked up on his struggles when I noticed he couldn't sleep any more than three hours during the night, if that. However, I ignored the warning signs.

We got married in January 2011, and I was pregnant with my world, the love of my life, my baby girl. The day I found out that I was pregnant, my husband was on a plane, flying to a location to fight for his country. Around seven months into my pregnancy, he called me to tell me that a month before we got married he had cheated on me and that she would be due around September. I couldn't believe what I heard. The next thing that came out of his mouth put a bad taste in my mouth and filled me with hate. hate. He told me that he had waited till I was far along in my pregnancy to tell me what he did, so that I wouldn't be able to get an abortion. I was hurt and my trust in him was gone.

My husband returned from his deployment in November 2011, right before our daughter was born. He returned different; a shell of his old self. It was like whatever he had seen on his deployment had taken something from him. His nightmares kept him from sleeping and he began to drink more. On New Year's Eve, he said he was going out with his friends, leaving me home with a newborn. At 2 a.m. I heard a knock at the door. One of my husband's friends drove his car home to tell me that my husband had been arrested for DUI. I had to pack up my less than three-week-old baby to go bail her dad out of jail! I was upset and just fed up with the nonsense.

By May 2013, my job sent me to Texas and my husband had been medically retired from the military. I thought life would get better, but it was a downhill nightmare! He stopped taking his prescribed medication and started smoking synthetic drugs. The day I couldn't take it anymore was the day he stood over me and said he could throw me down the steps and burn my body on the grill. At that point, I wasn't going to give him a chance to show me. I waited for him to fall asleep. Then I grabbed my baby and left the house to call the sheriff. I couldn't believe that the hospital only kept him for 72 hours! We were on a slippery slope and I couldn't allow our daughter to live like that anymore.

God made a way for me, and my child, and when I thought I couldn't make it on my own, I prayed about it. I went through so much in my second marriage. What I thought was love, was just words with no meaning. I was a victim of domestic violence and still suffer from its long-term effects. There is much more to my story, but that's for another book!

Throughout my failed marriage and *love* I have come out stronger than before and with great determination to keep going. God gave me the strength to walk away from two unhealthy marriages that were not rooted in real, respectful *love*. I walked away with no regrets. My *love* journey has not made me bitter, it has made me *wiser*.

Love Notes:

Love Notes:

Author Sandra Williams

Author Sandra Williams

Born and raised most of her childhood in the small rural town of Roxobel, North Carolina, in Bertie County, Sandra Williams (McGlone) is now a resident of Youngsville, North Carolina. She is the second oldest of six girls (one deceased-Temperance) born to an amazing mother, Geraldine Cherry of Roxobel, North Carolina.

Sandra Williams is the mother of two boys, Anthony Quamaine Whitaker and Deonta' Kenyon Whitaker, both deceased. She was married to Barry McGlone (deceased) for nine and a half years. She has an awesome, intelligent, beautiful granddaughter, Jammie Whitaker who resides with her mother, Chezley. Sandra also has four God-daughters Zoe'Bishop-Bridgers, Jakhia Basnight, Aaliyah Hall, and Kahlay Bishop.

Sandra earned her high school diploma with the Class of 1988 from Bertie High School, Windsor, North Carolina. Sandra continued her education at Shaw University, Raleigh, North Carolina, earning a Bachelor of Arts Degree in Social Work (Magna Cum Laude), with a Minor in Special Education. She earned a Master's in Secondary Education -Curriculum and Instruction (Magna Cum Laude) from the University of Phoenix- Phoenix, Arizona and completed her North Carolina licensure program in School Social Work at North Carolina State University, Raleigh, North Carolina.

In her present role as a Licensed School Social Worker at Vance County Middle School, Henderson, North Carolina, Sandra is an experienced, educated, energetic individual who believes in helping families and children in meeting their needs educationally and at home. Through referrals to community agencies, and providing parenting skills through Triple P Parenting (Positive Parenting Program) she positively impacts the lives of those she serves. Sandra has served many roles in the educational sector over the course of her twenty-three years in education. Wearing many hats, these roles include: Seventh Grade Social Studies/Science Teacher, Driver Education Instructor, Front Office

Assistant, Bus Driver, Athletic Trainer, Multi-Tiered System of Supports team member- formerly known as School Base Team, Peer Mediation Facilitator, Truancy Team Member, School Testing Coordinator, Junior BETA Sponsor, and Cheerleader Coach (Football and Basketball). She also serves currently as the Parent Representative on the Child Fatality Prevention Team for Bertie County.

Sandra was also a Social Worker for Child Protective Services as an Investigation- Assessment- Treatment agent (ITA) at the Northampton County Department of Social Services, Jackson, North Carolina. As a Social Worker, her desire to ensure children were in a safe, nurturing, and caring environment pushed her to a focus-driven, supportive, and ambitious seven-year career in the North Carolina Department of Social and Human Services Child Protective Service Unit.

In addition to her work experience, her love and passion spread into the community. Sandra's volunteer services allow her to provide parents with tools and skills to better themselves and their families. She provides training in interviewing skills, work etiquette, and resume development. Sandra supports members of the community in securing housing and food assistance and provides direct instruction to individuals who need assistance in understanding life issues. Active in other community projects, she assists in providing basic needs and food for the homeless; and providing meals to the elderly and disabled during the holiday seasons.

Sandra is currently the President of the North Carolina School Social Work Association, and a member of Zeta Phi Beta Sorority Incorporated, Grand Chapter Order of the Eastern Star, Prince Hall Affiliation- Past Matron Royal Star Number Six Zero Six District Five, Daughter and Actual Past Commandress of Shadid Court Number Two-Twelve Daughter of the Imperial Courts- An Auxiliary of the Ancient Egyptian Arabic Order of Nobles Mystic Shrine of North and South America and Its Jurisdictions, Incorporated. Also, she is a Loyal Lady Ruler of the Order of the Golden Circle, Prince Hall Affiliated.

Sandra's listing of her education, career, and community involvement tells what she does, but not who she belongs to. She is a member of the Heavenly Father's Family; she is a child of God! All her life, she has been a member of the Sandy Branch Missionary Baptist Church in Roxobel, North Carolina under the leadership of Reverend Ricardo

Hardison, Senior, where she serves as a Church Clerk, Worship Leader Committee member, Hostess Committee member, Public Relation Committee member and Vacation Bible School Coordinator-Facilitator. Sandra continues to hold her faith in the God she knows, who has brought her through the tragedies of life that she has experienced. She shares through her smile, work, and faith that God is all you need in this world in which we live.

Focused on This Christian Walk:
A Concluding Commentary

God has already written the forecast in our lives, and He is holding the umbrella for the rainstorms, the pain, the sleepless nights, the frustration, the tragedies, the sickness, and the times we will get off track. God knows where our steps are going to take us. For each step we must complete in this course, there is something we will encounter. It may be a reward, consequence, pain, joy, or a lesson. God **will give you what you need to get through**, even when you feel like you are taking one step forward and two steps backward. While you are going through the steps, praise God. For the devil hates a Step-Praiser! So, for every step you take…. praise him! Just praise him for everything and you will find that step getting a little easier, that load a little lighter, those tasks, and duties of a good child of God, working themselves out. The devil sees you, knows what you are doing and going through, and will say- "*Why don't you just give up?*" Sandra says, "*God is here to tell you to press towards the mark of the high calling.*" For, she is a believer that the more you recognize who you are, and whose you are, the less you are willing to be who you were.

Email address: Sandyoumay.swm@gmail.com
Facebook: sandrawilliams
Instagram: sandyoumay

A Transitioning Walk Without YOU...

My Heart, My Love, My Joy...
(Anthony, Deonta,' & Barry)

You don't know my story,
All the things that I've been through,
You can't feel my pain,
What I had to go through to get here,
You'll never understand my Praise...
I've been through too much...
-Bishop Larry Trotter

I remember the days when I would count the months, weeks, days, hours, minutes, seconds since I last heard your voice, hugged you, laid eyes on the physical human part of you, laughed with you, kissed you, or said, "*I love you*!" You see, my dear children and husband, there have been some difficult, lonely, and praying days since you have been gone. Most of all, there have been days of rejoicing about how your lives touched so many. Now, I pray and rejoice as I move along the way of this transitioning walk into a predestined life that I never considered walking in.

Throughout our life, we transition through many things. We go through life experiencing rewards, consequences, obstacles, and even tragedies based on our actions. Both good deeds and bad decision-making can create abrupt changes in our life. If you have not experienced any of these life transitions, just wait a little while longer and I guarantee you, they will come. Most of the time we do not understand why things happen the way they do. Just know that one day, someway, somehow, it will be revealed to you why you are going through the transitions of life alone, but *NOT* alone.

Andre' Crouch said it best for me on the days after my loved ones left our dear family and departed from this world...

"I've had many tears and sorrows, I've had questions for tomorrow, ... but in every situation, God gave me a blessed consolation, that my trials come to only make me strong. Through it all, through it all, I've learned to trust in Jesus, I've learned to trust in God. I've learned to depend upon His word."

Even when I did not understand, did not know how or when I was going to get through the losses, I made it with the help of my JESUS, my family, my Church Family, and true friends.

You see, I have been through heavy obstacles in my life... On June Eighth, Twenty Thirteen, I woke up that morning thinking, "*Oh, what a wonderful day this is going to be*! I finally get to see my baby, Deonta', walk across the stage and receive his high school diploma! Even though that day, the day I never saw coming as the last day, was the day that was about to start me on a new transition in life, I still count it as a *Wonderful Day*.

Before leaving home, on that Saturday morning, I had talked to both my sons, Anthony and Deonta', expressing to them how proud I was of them, and their accomplishments in life. I did something most mothers do not get to do, tell their children, "*I love you*", not realizing it is for the final time!

I told Anthony how proud I was of him for stepping up, working, caring, and being a supportive father for his daughter, Jammie. I said to him, "*Obstacles will hit you in the face at some point in life. Do not let your obstacles or tragedies dictate or define you, who you are going to be, or even what you are going to do in life. Let your obstacles and tragedies be a stepping stone to the doorway of life's opportunities. Let life experiences be a part of your learning, and Your Master be your guide. For he knows all, and He cares. You see Anthony, this life will not always be peaches and cream, or a bed of roses. I want you to KNOW that life is not full of complications and misfortune, however, whatever is the Master's plan, it will be.* Anthony told me, "*Mom, I love you and thank you for being there for me, thank you for being the Great Mom steering me in the right direction. I know I may not have done everything you wanted me to do, but I love you and I appreciate you.*"

Repeatedly, I think about the day Deonta' was born with a heart condition that required heart surgery within his first week of life, and then at three months, and again at seven months. And now, that very day, the day of his high school graduation, June Eighth, Twenty Thirteen was here. I also talked to Deonta' on that very morning, not knowing it would be my last morning with my baby, My Miracle Child! I told him, *"Life is full of ups and downs, sadness and happiness, laughter, and tears, but with God on your side, all these things are doable and possible in life."* Often, I remember how Deonta' would ask, *"Why do I have to take this class?"* Yet, on that day, I remember that Deonta', you came to me, hugged me, and kissed me on my jaw, and said, *"Mommy, thanks for pushing me, thanks for making me take those classes. Thanks, Mommy, for staying on me and making me do the things I was supposed to do. Thanks for being a Great Mom and caring about my future."* Deonta', you said to me, "I know it may seem like I did not appreciate what you were telling me, but Mom, I was listening. I was paying attention and I am thankful."

Hey, My Babies… Mommy remembers the big splatter-kisses on my cheeks that the both of you gave me at the same time before I walked out the door. Our conversations together on that day helped me each and every day since you left this world. I miss you so much!!!

I remember sitting in the gym when the Principal, Mr. Calvin Moore, walked over to me and told me he wanted to see me. I remember walking out of the gym and seeing the Sheriff, Deputies,

Police Officers, Staff, Superintendent Elaine White, Board Members, and others standing there with such sad faces. I remembered being told that my children were not going to be at graduation because of an accident they were involved in. I remembered when I was told that they had been killed! I remembered asking the questions, *"Lord, why? What have I done to deserve this?"* Many nights later, God answered my questions in a dream. He said, *"They were not your children, they were mine! I loaned them to you for a short time to love, care for, and nurture their lives to be examples of the type of young men I need in these last days of this world. You have done just that!"* It was after that dream that I realized all this was predestined in my life. I did not understand why, but I knew I had to continue to run on for My God. I had always been told by my Mom, *"God makes no mistakes. If he brought you to it, He will bring you through it!"* I had to just believe her words. And trust God.

Yes, there are times when people say, *"How do you do this?"* I tell them, *"It's the strength of God!"* I want you to know it is only God who strengthens me and it's only because of Him I can go through this part of my life. It's a daily walk with God. This predetermined destiny and purpose are why I can share my walk, my steps, my ups, and my downs, and I can tell you He is an Amazing God!

Not one day since June Eighth, Twenty Thirteen, have I not thought of my children. Not one day do I regret raising them the way I did. Not one day that I am not thankful for having told my children on that day, "*I love you. You are The Best Children a Mom could ever have!*"

Then, another obstacle showed itself on March Fourth, Twenty Eighteenth. I returned home to find my husband, Barry, dead on the kitchen floor of our home! My husband was a person whom I had known basically all my adult life. Now he was gone! My pain was great and I cried out, *"How do I go on? How do I move into this new walk of life without you? I don't know what you're doing Lord, but I need your help! Help in fighting for what was rightfully mine, or just giving it up and walking away! Lord, I don't understand how this is happening to me, yet again. I'm losing someone who was a part of my life for so very long. Married for almost ten years, friends for even longer, my husband is now gone! Was there enough time to put things in place? Barry, why didn't you do what we talked about? Planned for? I saw the Last Will and Testament come in the mail; we talked about it. You said, "It's taken care of, and you don't have to worry about anything." Why didn't I look at all things? I didn't because I trusted in your word. I don't get it! I just don't get it!"*

So now Chakakan and Deshelle have gone home, after supporting me for over two weeks, and I've said, *"I'm okay"* when I am really not. So, I turned to my doctor for more meds to help me sleep at night because I am pacing the floor, trying to figure it out. Sleeping for only two to three hours a night because now I am truly alone. **But God...** Calling my mom, Geraldine, in the wee hours of the morning, asking my Auntie Mildred for prayer daily, calling my

BFFs, Warren and Regina to vent, cry, or just hold the phone because I felt I needed someone there to help me get over this stone in my pathway, on the rocky road I am walking down. Barry, what about your friend, Gus- supporting when and where he could? I am truly grateful for talks with my sisters, Martine, Amanda, Genet, and Yvette who called in the midst of caring for themselves and their families. **But God…**

Remembering the good days when we traveled by air, land, and water, sharing in moments of love, happiness, and joy, sustains me. Barry, we shared our life together and especially felt blessed by the birth of our grandchildren. I saw your kindhearted actions to protect Jammie's health and to ensure that she was okay. You enjoyed the opportunity to babysit the grandchildren even when you could have been expected to be worrying or concentrating on your medical report of prostate cancer. You wanted to put off your treatment because you said, "*The grandchildren are coming soon.*"

We used to have many conversations about the joys and barriers in your quest to become a Bertie County Schools Board Member. I remember the talks about how we felt Mr. Otis Smallwood would be a great Superintendent for Bertie County Schools. Well, guess what Barry, your desired wish has come true! I look back on the Football Championship Games you coached, standing out on the field in shorts like you were not cold! When you knew it was thirty-two degrees or below outside! I often reflect on how good of a drummer you were. I passed along your personal equipment to Mike Cherry (aka your nephew). I'm sure Mount Olive Missionary Baptist Church misses the best drummer they ever had. There will never be another Barry the Drummer! I laid your body to rest in the right spot, in the church cemetery, just in case you needed to hear the beat of the drums.

Reflecting on our proposal, I remember chuckling at you when you told me that on Monday, September Fifth, Two Thousand Eleven, you got locked in the Ultra Diamonds with the store manager, trying to get my engagement ring, in the midst of Tropical Storm Lee. Then how you planned to propose to me on the plane but was scared because 911 had just occurred. Barry, I hold to my heart, to my God, through all the pain, confusion, and disappointments I have been through since you left. Even in the midst of memories built together, we shared a healer, deliver, joy, and love; we shared God! We shared a peace between us like no other, when it came to God. We could talk about the Word of God and disagree, but agree. But we both said, and knew that God can and will do exceedingly, abundantly in all things that are designed for us and around us.

Throughout my life, I have been through a lot of transitions; some of which appeared to me to be harder than others, but through them all, with God on my side, I have made it. Even when I did not understand, didn't know how or when I was going to get through, *I made it.*

A tragedy!!!!!! Know that when something happens in life you don't get the answer to the *why* in that minute, hour, day, week month or perhaps even that year. However, one day, your *Why* will be answered. Tragedies come but will never take away a lifetime of memories!!!

One day, after burying my children, I was cleaning out Deonta's closet and book bag and I found this note. The note read...

> **On July Seventh, 1995, at approximately 3:45 a.m. my first cry out for air was recorded. As I opened my eyes and looked around the room I had no clue who any of the people in the room were, but this one woman I glanced at, it seemed that I knew exactly who she was. Her touch seemed so common that I knew who she was instantly. I would later call her Mommy. As the doctor examined my infant body, he realized that I was born with a very rare heart disease at the time. The cardiovascular disease that I was also born with caused me to have three holes in my heart. I needed surgery immediately. Being that I was not supposed to live, the doctors pulled through a miracle.**

Who am I? I am Deonta' Kenyon Whitaker. The son of Sandra Williams and Danny Whitaker. I am a seventeen-year-old young man with an extremely bright and promising future. Life, to me, is a beautiful thing to be cherished. You are fortunate enough to have a life with your parents.

My look on the future job is healthy. I believe I will be one of the top guys in the Military. I want to be the person who others inform me that something really tragic has happened. In conclusion, I am a young man with a very bright and promising future. My advice to everyone who reads this is, make the best of your life while you can. Spread peace and love to everyone, because in this cruel world we all need it.

~ Deonta' Kenyon Whitaker

Because through it all,
through it all,
I've learned to trust in Jesus
I've learned to depend upon his word...

You don't know my story,
You can't feel my pain,
I've been through too much
Anthony, Deonta', Barry
My Heart, My Love, My Joy...
A Transitioning Walk without YOU ....

Love Notes:

ABOUT THE VISIONARY:
Author Michelle Dowleyne

ABOUT THE VISIONARY:
Author Michelle Dowleyne

Michelle Dowleyne is a motivational speaker, bestselling author, founder of a 501c3 nonprofit organization *Boots 2 Heels, Inc.* and Visionary of the successful book compilations, *Her Story is My Story* and *Love Chronicles*. She enjoys reading, spending time with her family, and relaxing. Michelle has been married to Daryl Dowleyne for over seven years. They have three children: Sharice, Daunte, and Nijia, one grandson, Daryl, and a beautiful granddaughter, Kennedy.

She received her Bachelor's Degree in Psychology from Cameron University. She received her Master's Degree in Business Administration from Strayers University and she graduated with honors.

In March 2012, Michelle was diagnosed with Major Depression and Post Traumatic Stress Disorder. Despite these disabilities, she follows the lead of God and serves women by empowering them through her ministry. Her vision came to fruition in March 2020, during the pandemic. As a result of her own personal struggles, Michelle derived her drive for helping others and this has become her passion. If she can help one person, by sharing her story, then the healing process begins. She is now showing other co-authors how to share their stories to bless others. Michelle believes her disability is not a setback but a blessing that enables her to help others seek self-awareness and empowerment.

Michelle loves God and believes He guides her path. Being actively involved in her community, she spends a lot of time volunteering. She believes that we live in communities where we can see the development of more powerful and successful women being a resource to each other and to the community instead of being a liability. Michele reminds us to- *"Believe in yourself and all that you are. Know that there is something inside you that is greater than any obstacle."* Christian D. Larson shero publishing

Made in the USA
Middletown, DE
02 November 2021